Sentence Diagramming

A Step-by-Step Approach to Learning Grammar Through Diagramming

Sentence Diagramming

A Step-by-Step Approach to Learning Grammar Through Diagramming

Marye Hefty • Sallie Ortiz • Sara Nelson

PEARSON
Longman

New York   San Francisco   Boston
London   Toronto   Sydney   Tokyo   Singapore   Madrid
Mexico City   Munich   Paris   Cape Town   Hong Kong   Montreal

Acquisitions Editor: Melanie Craig

Marketing Manager: Thomas DeMarco

Senior Supplements Editor: Donna Campion

Supplements Editor: Jenna Egan

Production Manager: Stacey Kulig

Project Coordination, Text Design, and Electronic Page Makeup: Pre-Press Company, Inc.

Cover Design Manager: Wendy Ann Fredericks

Cover Designer: Nancy Sacks

Manufacturing Manager: Mary Fischer

Printer and Binder: Command Web Offset Co.

Cover Printer: Coral Graphics Services

Copyright © 2008 by Pearson Education, Inc.

Please visit us at www.ablongman.com

ISBN 10: 0-205-55126-2

ISBN 13: 978-0-205-55126-2

2 3 4 5 6 7 8 9 10—BRR—10 09 08 07

CONTENTS

Preface

Introduction xi

Chapter One
The Eight Parts of Speech 1

Chapter Two
Crafting the Simple Sentence 5

Chapter Three
Constructing the Compound Sentence 37

Chapter Four
Building the Complex Sentence 45

Chapter Five
Pronouns. 69

Chapter Six
Verbals 87

Chapter Seven
Verbs 99

Appendix
Diagrams for Practice 125

Index 191

Dedication

This book is dedicated to the teachers in our lives who had the energy, commitment, and insight to teach us basic skills, even when doing so was not in vogue.

Acknowledgments

We are thankful to our families and friends for their support. We are grateful to Nathan Harden for his sentence examples and intellectual curiosity, which provided needed inspiration. Deniece Davis, a skilled library technician, shared our passion for reviving sentence diagramming, and she helped us find and enjoy treasures like Alonzo Reed and Brainerd Kellogg's 1876 and 1889 books, *Graded Lessons in English*. Carol Wylie, one of the teachers referred to in our dedication, carefully reviewed our manuscript and provided invaluable suggestions for our revision. Melanie Craig and Frederick Speers at Longman Publishers and Lindsay Mateiro at Pre-Press Company led us skillfully through the publication process. We are thankful to the students, like John and Lisa Najar, whose questions show us what is clear and what is not, and whose enthusiasm for learning reminds us why our book was worth the effort.

In a few instances, we cite Mark Lester's textbook *Grammar and Usage in the Classroom*. We could find no other sources for this cited information, and we believe that these are author-specific ideas and not general knowledge.

Preface

By Marye Hefty

Before the 1960s, grammar and punctuation were taught as foundation blocks for writing instruction. In the 1960s, some research questioned the value of teaching grammar, and new ways of teaching grammar cast doubt on the traditional methods. In the midst of all of this change, the baby was thrown out with the bath water where grammar was concerned, and when the 1970s rolled around, a new generation of teachers had not been trained to teach grammar and punctuation.

I am a member of that new generation of teachers, and a product of a writing education with little structured or sustained lessons in grammar. Thankfully, one of my teachers believed in teaching grammar and punctuation through sentence diagramming. Before this instruction, I lacked confidence in my writing because I didn't know for sure if my sentences were really sentences.

I can still remember the great "aha!" feeling I had when I realized that I could analyze a sentence without the teacher's assistance—I could mentally diagram the sentence to determine if it was grammatically correct. What a sense of power that gave me!

After graduating college with a master's degree in English, I became a professional editor for a research laboratory. During my time in that position, I learned from experienced technical editors how to edit in depth for meaning, clarity, flow, and conciseness. I also edited for grammar and punctuation, but I still felt woefully inept at quoting the rules to explain some of the grammar changes I made to my authors' papers. I would often forget the rules I had painstakingly looked up in grammar handbooks from one assignment to the next because they didn't seem to be part of an overall structure that I could remember.

When an author asked me when to use the word "myself" and when to use the word "me," I didn't know the answer. I realized then that I had to find a tool that would enable me to learn grammar and punctuation well without having to commit endless rules to memory. I remembered the confidence I had felt years earlier using sentence diagramming to learn and explain grammar, and I began looking for a sentence diagramming book.

My search for a good sentence diagramming book began in the mid-1980s before access to the Internet, online libraries, and Amazon.com. I used an old-fashioned approach to finding information—asking peers and combing the library, and initially I did not find any book dedicated to teaching grammar by diagramming. Finally, an editor I worked with who was near retirement gave me a copy of an out-of-print 1933 book entitled *The Mastery of the Sentence*, by Dorothy Dakin. What a treasure I found in this book! I used it to regain my basic competence with diagrams. I could also see the need for a more complete and modern version of a sentence diagramming book for teaching the functions and vocabulary of the English language to students today. This sparked my motivation for researching and writing this book.

When I left the research laboratory to become a college professor, teaching English composition and technical writing, I noticed during the first term that many of my students' papers were riddled with grammar and punctuation errors. I didn't know how to add the necessary instruction in grammar and punctuation skills to our limited class time without letting it take over the class like a weed. Typically, I tried a band-aid approach to teaching grammar and punctuation. When I saw sentence fragments in the students' papers, I talked about sentence fragments. When I saw comma splices, I talked about those. It didn't take long to realize that many of my students didn't recognize a sentence, so they couldn't solve the sentence problems. My students were just like I had been—needing structure and an organized way to learn grammar and punctuation without having the approach overwhelm them or make it difficult for them to learn the writing process in class.

In several classes, I decided to discard the band-aid approach and devote 10 percent of the class time to teaching the students grammar and punctuation, starting with the basics—What is a simple sentence? How do you diagram it? And guess what? It worked.

I've been teaching sentence diagramming in some of my courses for eight years now, and the students who begin my classes not being able to identify or define a simple sentence leave the class with the vocabulary and knowledge to identify simple, compound, and complex sentences; fragments; run-ons; and comma splices. Most importantly, the students have a foundation that enables them to learn more—without my help—after they leave the class.

Surprisingly, my university students don't mind having to learn grammar and punctuation through sentence diagramming because this approach quickly gives them the skills and confidence to fix the problems in their papers on their own. I have heard enough anecdotal evidence from my students to know that sentence diagramming works. For example, one of my former students told me that she was asked to edit letters for her boss. She said that before taking my class, she just put the commas in where she thought she heard a pause and just guessed that the sentences were correct. "Now I know for sure, and I can really help," she said.

Introduction

For the Teacher

The value of using sentence diagramming to teach grammar and punctuation is that it is a visual method of teaching, and visual learners constitute over 70 percent of our population. This book, *Sentence Diagramming*, provides a structured, visual, and step-by-step approach to learning about language that is not overwhelming to the student. It builds a natural path through the forest of language rules. This book provides a framework for remembering the rules and concepts and helps students to rely on their own analytical abilities as editors.

Nothing is more tedious for students than having to look up and memorize language rules. Diagramming makes this process seem like a game of strategy, much like chess. It provides a common and internalized vocabulary for language and helps the student look at language with a bit more depth.

The special organization of this book is by design to give students specific information as they need it. The organization starts with the simple basics, beginning with the parts of speech—assuming that the learner knows very little about English grammar. Then the book builds, step by step, on information that can be immediately used by the student to master the rules of grammar.

Students can easily become mired in grammar details before they know how to solve any problems with their new grammar knowledge; therefore, early in the book, diagramming is used to show students how subjects must agree in number with their verbs, and that the objects of prepositional phrases cannot be the subjects of sentences. With this knowledge, the student can easily solve many different subject/ verb agreement problems.

This book also teaches the grammar lessons in a logical sequence; for example, instead of teaching all the details of pronouns in one chapter, the basic definition and use of a pronoun is taught first, along with the other parts of speech. With this preliminary knowledge, the student can learn basic grammar rules involving pronouns. Later, when the student is ready to learn the details of pronouns, the book teaches which pronouns to use as subjects and which to use as objects.

The organization of this book is a bit like a good wilderness guide—taking students along paths that gradually require increased effort as they are prepared to experience them. In this way, students feel a sense of accomplishment in their newly acquired skills and look forward to adding to their knowledge. This book also guides teachers in how to use sentence diagramming to teach grammar. By simply studying one section ahead of the students, the teacher will have a fully prepared lesson plan.

Specifically, the book is organized as follows:

Chapter 1: The Eight Parts of Speech. This chapter provides the basic definitions needed to begin diagramming.

Chapter 2: Crafting the Simple Sentence. This chapter defines a simple sentence and shows how the eight parts of speech are diagrammed within sentences. Next, this chapter defines and uses diagrams to show how the parts of speech can have many special functions within sentences. Specifically, the chapter defines and shows the uses of direct objects, indirect objects, subjective complements, objectives complements, appositives, and nouns of address. Through defining and showing the parts and functions of speech, this chapter logically teaches the rules related to basic subject/verb agreement and comma use in multiple adjectives.

Chapter 3: Constructing the Compound Sentence. This chapter defines the compound sentence and shows the three ways to properly punctuate such a sentence: using a semicolon, using a comma with a coordinating conjunction, and using a conjunctive adverb preceded by a semicolon and followed by a comma.

Chapter 4: Building the Complex Sentence. This chapter defines the complex sentences and the three types of dependent clauses: adjective, adverb, and noun clauses. Through diagramming, the chapter defines and shows when to use *who, whom, that,* and *which;* how to punctuate the adverb clause; how to identify sentence fragments in adverb clauses; and how to ensure subject/verb agreement in the noun clause.

Chapter 5: Pronouns. This chapter defines and shows how to properly use subjective and objective case pronouns. It also covers the proper use of possessive case, reflective, intensive, indefinite, demonstrative, relative (review from Chapter 4), interrogative, and reciprocal pronouns.

Chapter 6: Verbals. This chapter defines and shows how to properly use the three types of verbals: participle, gerund, and infinitive, including how to avoid dangling participles.

Chapter 7: Verbs. This restates verb concepts defined in previous chapters, such as the difference between action and linking verbs. The chapter reviews subject/ verb agreement. New topics include understanding passive and active voice and properly using verbs in the subjunctive mood. Finally, the chapter provides reference information related to the forms and tenses of verbs.

For the Student

Sentence Diagramming teaches a streamlined approach to learning sentence vocabulary. This book provides a structured step-by-step method of learning about the sentence, a framework for remembering rules and concepts, and a common vocabulary for talking about language. You'll learn the functions of words within simple, compound, and complex sentences.

This book uses sentence diagramming to teach the basic rules of grammar and punctuation, and it will help you identify and solve common sentence problems like fragments, run-on sentences, and comma splices. The diagrams are used to train you to review and analyze language instead of simply memorizing rules. As a result, you will be able to use diagrams to look at sentences in depth.

The language vocabulary and tools in this book will give you the foundation to understand what the teacher is teaching. For example, when the teacher states that a group of words is a "fragment," you will be able to use diagramming to analyze the group of words to see why it is a fragment.

"He who would write clearly ought first to think clearly."

– Goethe

This book provides a logical map for framing the rules of grammar within an overall structure (i.e., it identifies the forest from the trees), which is essential for long-term comprehension and application when you leave school.

The instructions in this book build step by step and connect logically to enable you to easily see how the information is connected, providing you with a framework in which to learn new information. The book shows you how to use diagrams to solve specific grammar or punctuation problems. This approach is analogous to describing how to solve a math problem and then giving an example of a real-life problem that can be solved using your newly acquired diagramming skill.

The foundation skills taught in this book are designed to increase your confidence in writing. When you see that you can identify sentence problems within your own writing and fix them, you will be more confident about your writing skills and therefore your ability to communicate ideas clearly.

Sentence diagramming allows you to become actively involved in learning how to improve your own writing. Instead of relying on the teacher to point out the errors after you have turned in your paper, you become trained as a self-editor who continually looks for ways to improve your own writing.

What This Book Does Not Teach

Diagramming cannot be used to analyze every sentence problem in the English language—especially extremely complex sentences. However, the information in this book can be used to help you identify and analyze most sentences. Also, this book does not cover every grammar and punctuation rule and every exception. It does, however, cover the major rules and concepts that will give you the foundation for discovering and understanding new rules and concepts.

Because this book begins at the beginning and covers the basics, it can be used even more effectively with other language resources.

Chapter 1

The Eight Parts of Speech

Sentence diagramming is a tool you can use to make learning grammar and punctuation like learning to play an intriguing and thoughtful game—such as chess, for example. Instead of attempting to memorize endless lists of unrelated rules, you first need to recognize the eight parts of speech and learn their functions—just as you would first learn the names and functions of chess pieces when learning to play the game of chess.

> ## Learning Objectives for Chapter 1
>
> After studying this chapter, you will be able to
>
> • Define the eight parts of speech

In this book, you will begin at the beginning, first learning to recognize the eight parts of speech and their functions within a simple sentence before moving on to the next level. The chapters in this book and the practice lessons in the workbook will guide and introduce you to levels of detail about the parts of speech and grammar rules as you need to learn them.

The definitions provided here are basic, so you will not get bogged down in the heavy details of grammar and will move forward in the learning process. Later chapters will discuss, for example, the types of pronouns and verbs. Also, rules related to specific parts of speech will be introduced when they will help you most to understand the application of a diagramming concept or a grammar or punctuation rule.

But for now, you will simply begin at the beginning.

All words can be classified into the following eight parts of speech:

▶ 1. Noun
— a word used to name a person, place, idea, or thing

> The old *cowboy* and his *horse* rode into town on *Sunday*.

▶ 2. Pronoun
— a word used in place of a noun

> *He* rode the horse because *they* liked Sunday afternoon rides.

▶ 3. Verb

— a word used to express action (play, sing, study) or being (is, are, be, become).

> The cowboy *rode* and *talked* while the horse simply *walked*.

> The cowboy and the horse *are* good friends.

▶ 4. Adjective

— a word used to modify or describe a noun or a pronoun. An adjective usually answers one of these questions: Which one? How many? What kind?

> The *gentle* horse listened to the *lengthy* stories of the *old* cowboy.

Articles

— also classified as adjectives. These three words ("a," "an," and "the") are used to introduce nouns.

> *An* old cowboy and his horse stopped at *the* ice cream parlor for *a* sarsaparilla.

▶ 5. Adverb

— a word used to modify a verb, an adjective, or another adverb. It usually answers one of these questions:

- **When?**

> The horse walks *often*.

- **Where?**

> The horse walks *outside*.

- **How?**

> The horse walks *carefully* over the sharp rocks.

- Why? or under what conditions?

> The horse eats carrots *because she loves them*. (adverbial clause)

- To what degree?

> The horse is *very* calm.

▶ 6. Preposition

—a word used to show the relation of a noun or a pronoun to another word in the sentence. The prepositional phrase almost always functions as an adjective or an adverb. Note that the preposition never is used alone but is always at the beginning of a phrase that ends in a noun or pronoun.

> The cowboy rode *into* town *on* his horse.

One old trick you can use to identify most (but not all) prepositions is to see if the word fits logically into the blank space in the following sentence:

The cow jumped _____ the moon.

A LIST OF COMMON PREPOSITIONS					
about	before	concerning	like	over	under
above	behind	down	near	past	underneath
across	below	despite	next	plus	unlike
after	beneath	during	of	since	until
against	beside	except	off	than	unto
along	besides	for	on	through	with
among	between	from	onto	throughout	within
around	beyond	in	opposite	till	without
as	by	inside	out	to	
at	considering	into	outside	toward	

▶ 7. Conjunction

—a word used to join words, phrases, or clauses, and to indicate the relation between the elements joined. One type of conjunction is the coordinating conjunction, which includes *and, or, but, yet, so, nor,* and *for.* A mnemonic for remembering the coordinating conjunctions is "fanboys," which consists of the first letter of each conjunction.

The cowboy stopped at the general store to buy ice cream, *but* the horse stayed outside.

▶ 8. Interjection

—a word used to express surprise or emotion

Wow! The horse ate the cowboy's ice cream cone.

These eight parts of speech are your set of grammar game pieces. When you are able to identify and define these eight parts of speech, you can begin to diagram sentences and to use grammar and punctuation rules you may not have understood before.

The ability to identify the eight parts of speech within a simple sentence is absolutely essential in the game of sentence diagramming. In the game of chess, for example, if you don't know a rook from a pawn, you can't play the game.

Since it is essential for you to recognize the parts of speech and know their functions before you are able to diagram sentences, practice lessons are provided at the end of each section of this book. Please don't skip them.

"Knowledge is power."

– Sir Francis Bacon

Note: Volumes have been written about the details of the eight parts of speech. Because this book provides a step-by-step approach, this brief overview is enough to get you started diagramming. Once you have mastered simple diagramming concepts, more complex details are provided.

PRACTICE 1-1

Identify the part of speech indicated in **bold** in the following sentences. The answers are in the appendix.

1. **Knowledge** is power.—Sir Francis Bacon

2. **You** cannot teach a man anything; **you** can only help **him** find **it** within himself.—Galileo Galilei

3. I **hear** and I **forget**. I **see** and I **remember**. I **do** and I **understand**. —Confucius

4. The **important** thing is not to stop questioning.—Albert Einstein

5. If **the** English language made any sense, **a** catastrophe would be **an** apostrophe with fur.—Doug Larson

6. Think **wrongly**, if you please, but in all cases think for yourself. —Doris Lessing

7. Frederick Douglas taught that literacy is the path **from** slavery **to** freedom.—Carl Sagan

Note: As we will learn in the next chapter, the parts of speech can have different functions within a sentence, which can make learning grammar and diagramming a bit confusing at first. For example, "Knowledge is power" contains two nouns (knowledge, power) and a verb (is). In this sentence, the noun "power" functions as a subjective complement (specifically a predicate nominative), and "knowledge" functions as the subject of the sentence. Don't worry about learning these functions right now. You'll be learning more about them in the next chapter.

Chapter 2

Crafting the Simple Sentence

In this book, you will be learning about the three structures of sentences: simple, compound, and complex. A sentence will also fit within one of the following four categories, depending on its purpose:

- The declarative sentence makes a statement. "I love English." A declarative sentence is punctuated with a period.

- The imperative sentence issues requests or commands. "Love English!" An imperative sentence has an understood "you" as the subject. "[You] love English!" This sentence can be punctuated with either a period or exclamation point.

- The interrogative sentence asks a question. "Why do you love English?" An interrogative sentence is punctuated with a question mark.

- The exclamatory sentence makes an exclamation. "Mastery of English is power!" An exclamatory sentence is a declarative sentence with an exclamation point to provide emphasis.

> ### Learning Objectives for Chapter 2
>
> After studying this chapter, you will be able to
> - Define and recognize a simple sentence
> - Diagram the eight parts of speech
> - Apply correct subject-verb agreement in relation to subjects and prepositional phrases
> - Understand, diagram, and make correct grammar choices for direct objects, indirect objects, subjective complements, objective complements, appositive phrases, and nouns of address

What Makes a Sentence "Simple"?

A simple sentence contains one independent clause. An independent clause must contain the following:

1. at least one subject and a predicate (the verb and any modifiers or complements if necessary), and

2. a complete thought.

For example,

> John runs.

John is the subject and *runs* is the verb. The idea is complete, so no modifiers are needed to complete the sentence.

Now consider this example,

> John is smart.

John is the subject, *is* is the verb, and *smart* is the complement. The verb needs the complement to make the sentence a complete thought. *Smart* completes the thought so that these words meet all the criteria of a simple sentence. It is an independent clause containing a subject (*John*) and a predicate (the verb *is* and its complement *smart*), and together these words convey a complete thought.

Congratulations! You now have all the information you need to begin the grammar game of diagramming!

Diagramming Simple Sentences— Starting with the Parts of Speech

In this section, you will learn how to diagram simple sentences. Remember that a diagram is a visual version of a sentence—a picture, so to speak. It helps you see the way each word functions in the sentence.

Diagramming Nouns and Verbs

In this sentence, the noun is the subject of the sentence.

> *Jill* ran.

Step 1:

To start your diagram, draw a horizontal line with a vertical line dividing the horizontal line in half, as shown below:

Step 2:

Write the noun that is the subject of the sentence on the top left side of the vertical line and the verb on the top right side, as shown below:

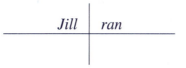

Jill | ran

Here are a few more examples:

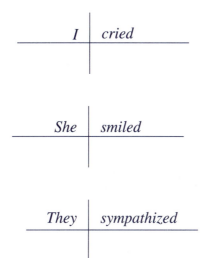

I | cried

She | smiled

They | sympathized

Diagramming Adjectives and Adverbs

This sentence contains an adjective, an adverb, and an article. Remember that articles are also classified as adjectives.

> *A light heart lives long.* –William Shakespeare

Step 1:

Start by diagramming the noun (subject of the sentence) and the verb as shown in the first example in Step 2 above:

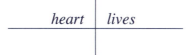

heart | lives

Step 2:

Now, draw diagonal lines under the noun for the article and adjective. Draw another diagonal line under the verb for the adverb (see example below). Note that visually the adjective and article are placed under the noun because they modify or describe it. The adverb is placed under the verb because it modifies or describes it.

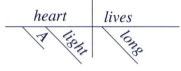

> **Template**
>
> Template for diagramming adjectives, articles, and adverbs.
>
> subject (noun) | verb
> article adjective | adverb

PRACTICE 2-1

Now try these sentences. You can check your work in the appendix.

1. The cold weather turned warm.

2. The dry snow fell slowly.

3. A small mouse ran quickly.

4. The good student studied hard.

5. The unhappy child cried softly.

If you are struggling to diagram these basic forms of simple sentences, this probably means that you have not yet mastered identifying the basic parts of speech. Before you continue, please review Chapter 1.

Diagramming Prepositional Phrases

Before you begin this section, memorize the list of common prepositions in Chapter 1.

Prepositions are found only as part of the prepositional phrase. A prepositional phrase consists of a preposition and its object (plus any modifiers of this object). The object of a preposition must be a noun or a pronoun.

The following are examples of prepositional phrases. The preposition is bolded and the object is italicized. The words between the preposition and the object are the modifiers.

by the *lake*

into the yellow *car*

to the *tailor*

with the energetic *students*

over the steep *mountain*

under the *sea*

Prepositional phrases are always modifiers within a sentence, and they modify either nouns or verbs. When they modify nouns, they are known as adjective prepositional phrases. When they modify verbs, they are known as adverbial prepositional phrases.

In the example sentence below, the adjective prepositional phrase is bolded, and the adverbial prepositional phrase is italicized.

The red car **in the long driveway** belongs *to Bill*.

Now, let's diagram it.

Step 1:

Start as before—draw the horizontal and vertical lines and fill in the subject and the verb. Next, draw the diagonal lines under the subject for the article and the adjective, as you have already learned.

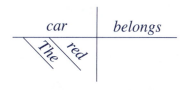

Step 2:

Now, here's what's new. For the adjective prepositional phrase, draw another diagonal line under the subject and then add a straight line to the end of it, sort of like a lazy L (see example). Put the preposition on the diagonal line and the object of the preposition on the straight line at the end. Follow the same approach for the adverbial prepositional phrase.

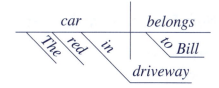

Step 3:

Add diagonal lines beneath the straight line of the object of the preposition for the article and adjective that modify the object of the preposition. See how easy this is when you know the parts of speech?

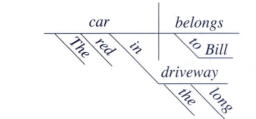

Template for diagramming prepositional phrases.

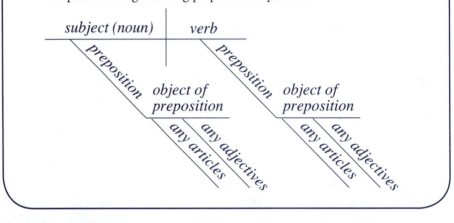

Try these sentences on your own. The answers are in the appendix.

1. The white car in the street belongs to my family.

2. His voice in the shower echoes throughout the house.

3. The explorer waded through knee-high snow.

4. The small dogs at the kennel crawled under the fence.

5. The experienced writer at the workshop spoke about his new book.

Diagramming Multiple Prepositional Phrases

This sentence contains two prepositions that both modify the same verb. The verb is **bolded,** the first prepositional phrase is *italicized*, and the second prepositional phrase is <u>underlined</u>.

We **trampled** *over the mud* <u>in our boots</u>.

Now what? No problem—just draw two lazy Ls under the verb, like this:

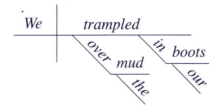

Now here is a tricky sentence with two prepositional phrases where one prepositional phrase modifies the verb and the other modifies the first prepositional phrase. The verb is **bolded,** the first prepositional phrase is *italicized,* and the second prepositional phrase is <u>underlined</u>.

> The boy **drank** *from the glass* <u>on the shelf</u>.

The prepositional phrase *from the glass* modifies the verb **drank**. However, the prepositional phrase <u>on the shelf</u> does not modify the verb **drank** because the boy didn't drink on the shelf. He **drank** *from the glass* <u>on the shelf</u>. *On the shelf* tells which glass the boy drank from, so <u>on the shelf</u> modifies *from the glass*.

Here is how you diagram a sentence with a prepositional phrase that modifies another prepositional phrase.

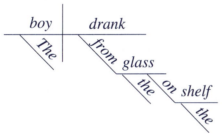

PRACTICE 2-3

1. The cat slept in the basket on the chair.

2. The newspaper landed on the porch of his house.

3. Subway trains in London travel in tunnels under the city.

4. The horse galloped through the field of wheat.

5. The girl swam in the lake at the foot of the mountain.

Diagramming to Determine Subject–Verb Agreement

In diagramming, with the actual subject and verb on the main line, it is easy to determine whether the verb agrees in number with the subject.

Here is a grammar problem you can solve with diagramming. Verbs must agree in number with their subjects.

For example,

> Five **students** *are* in the classroom, and ***one student*** *is* in the hallway.

> The **pilot** *flies* the plane, and the junior **pilots** *fly* the simulation.

Diagrams clearly illustrate if verbs agree in number with their subjects. Prepositional phrases tend to confuse the issue of subject-verb agreement if you do not remember that prepositional phrases are modifiers.

In diagramming, the prepositional phrase can't be placed on the main subject line or verb line because prepositions can't be subjects or verbs of a sentence. With the actual subject and verb on the main line, it is easy to determine whether the verb agrees in number with the subject.

The following are sentences that contain errors in subject-verb agreement that are difficult to recognize until the sentences are diagrammed. However, the errors are clearly visible within the diagrams.

> The **results** in the green notebook *shows* the problem.

results	show~~[s]~~

> The **advice** of three physical therapists *were* in the report.

advice	~~[were]~~ was

Rule

Remember that prepositional phrases are modifiers. The noun or pronoun of the phrase cannot be the subject or verb of the sentence. With the actual subject and verb in their proper places on the main diagramming line, it is easy to determine the correct subject-verb agreement.

Now, try diagramming the following sentences in order to make subject and verb agree. Remember that the verb must agree in number with the noun of the subject, not with the noun of the object in the prepositional phrase. Check your diagrams in the appendix.

1. Only one of the house lights (burn, burns) during the night.

2. The captain with his sailors (sail, sails) on the afternoon boat.

3. High levels of carbon monoxide (kill, kills) without warning.

4. A good set of professional golf clubs (cost, costs) about $500.

5. The rose with the carnations (is, are) in the vase.

Diagramming Multiple Nouns, Verbs, Adjectives, and Adverbs

A simple sentence will often have more than one noun, verb, adjective, or adverb. The term for more than one subject in a simple sentence is **compound subject**. More than one verb in a simple sentence is called a **compound verb**. Two or more adjectives and adverbs in a simple sentence are called **multiple adjectives** and **multiple adverbs**.

This section will teach you how to diagram these compound and multiple parts of speech in a simple sentence.

Compound Subjects

The following simple sentence contains a compound subject with two nouns (**bold**):

> The **cat** *and* **dog** ran swiftly.

Step 1:

Draw prongs for the compound subject on the left end of the horizontal base line, and draw the vertical subject-verb divider line to the right of the prongs, as shown in the diagram below. Place the first subject (**cat**) on the top prong line and the second subject (**dog**) on the bottom prong line. Draw a vertical dashed line between the two parts of the prong where it makes a V shape, and write the coordinating conjunction (*and*) on the dashed line as shown in the diagram.

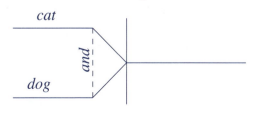

Step 2:

Now, finish the diagram.

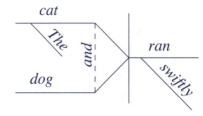

Let's try that again—this time with a sentence containing a compound subject (**bold**) and a prepositional phrase (*italic*), just to make it interesting.

The **man** and the **horse** walked *into town*.

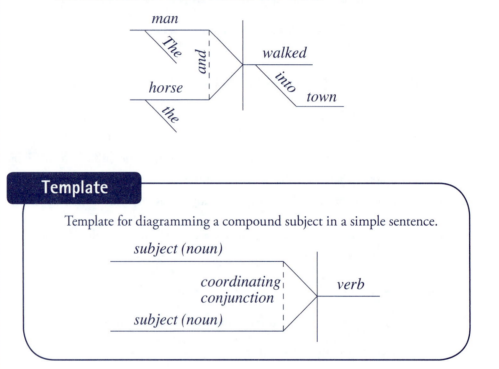

> **Template**
>
> Template for diagramming a compound subject in a simple sentence.
>
> subject (noun)
> coordinating conjunction
> subject (noun)
> verb

A compound subject can also contain three or more nouns. The simple sentence below contains a compound subject with three nouns (**bold**).

The fire **engine, ambulance**, and police **car** arrived at the accident.

To diagram a compound subject with three nouns, simply add a horizontal line within the prong as shown below:

If you are diagramming a sentence with even more subjects, you simply add as many lines within the prong as needed and write the subjects on the lines in the order in which they occur in the sentence.

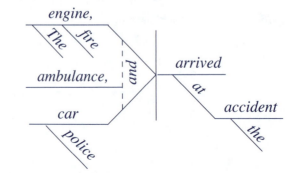

14 ©2008 by Marye Hefty, Sallie Ortiz, Sara Nelson

Now, try your growing diagramming skills on the following sentences containing compound subjects. Never fear—the answers are in the appendix.

1. The basketball players and their coach waited for the game.

2. The scorekeepers and the fans waited too.

3. The parents with young children and the tired grandparents went to their homes.

4. The head official and his assistant arrived after nine o'clock.

5. The girl, her father, and her mother waited in the airport.

Compound Verbs

The following simple sentence contains a compound verb (**bold**):

The cheetah **ran** swiftly and **jumped** quickly.

Step 1:

Draw the horizontal line for the subject and vertical line dividing the subject from the verb, and then draw the prong for the compound verb to the right of the vertical base line as shown in the diagram. Place the first verb (**ran**) on the top prong line and the second verb (**jumped**) on the bottom prong line.

Now, draw a vertical dashed line between the two parts of the prong where it makes a V shape, and write the coordinating conjunction (*and*) on the dashed line as shown in the diagram.

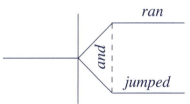

Step 2:

Now, finish the diagram.

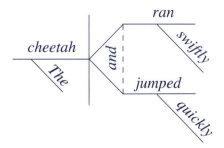

Template for diagramming compound verbs in a simple sentence.

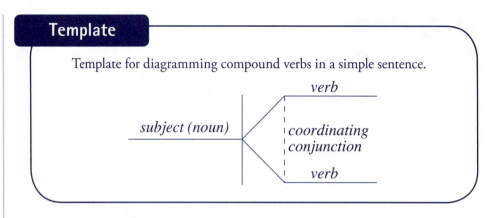

Sometimes one adjective or adverb in a sentence modifies both parts of a compound verb as in the sentence below:

She **ran** and **swam** swiftly.

Even though the modifier (*swiftly*), an adverb, modifies both the verbs **ran** and **swam**, the diagram should show the modifier (*swiftly*) placed on a diagonal line extending from the bottom prong line beneath the verb **swam**.

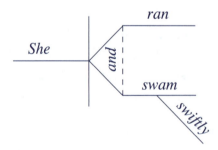

Compound verbs can also contain three or more verbs. The simple sentence below contains a compound verb with three verbs (**bold**), which are all modified by the adverb (swiftly).

The cheetah **ran**, **jumped**, and **swam** swiftly.

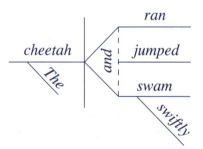

Now try diagramming compound verbs for yourself. You can check your answers in the appendix.

1. The cross-country runner jumped over the creek and ducked under the tree branch.

2. The seamstress measured with a yardstick and cut with fabric scissors.

3. The dog ran through the neighbor's yard and chased after the cat.

4. The student awoke early and studied for the test.

5. Five Lippizaner stallions pranced, danced, and jumped during their performance.

Multiple Adjectives

Multiple adjectives (*italic*) can modify the subject noun or pronoun (**bold**) as shown in the following simple sentence:

The *vast, rolling, golden* **fields** of grain stretched into the distance.

The adjectives (vast, rolling, and golden) all modify the subject (fields).

Step 1:

Draw the horizontal and vertical baselines. Place the subject (**fields**) to the left of the vertical baseline and the verb (*stretched*) to the right. Diagram the multiple adjectives (*vast, rolling, golden*) by placing each adjective on its own diagonal line beneath the subject (**fields**) in the order in which they appear in the sentence.

Step 2:

Now finish the diagram.

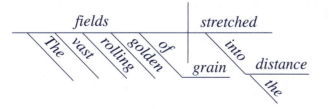

Template for diagramming multiple adjectives in a simple sentence.

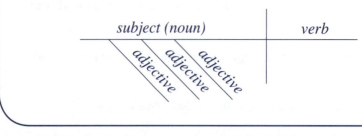

Rule

Placing Commas in Multiple Adjectives

Separate two or more adjectives by commas if each adjective equally modifies the same noun.

> Missy had always been a *faithful, loyal* dog.

The two adjectives are of equal rank if the comma can be replaced by the conjunction and without changing the sense of the sentence.

> Missy had always been a *faithful* and *loyal* dog.

Do not separate two adjectives by commas if the last adjective before the noun is part of an adjective/noun phrase, thereby outranking the preceding adjective.

> Her doghouse sat empty now beneath the *old* orange tree.

Orange tree is an adjective/noun phrase, and orange is more important than *old* in this case because orange can be considered part of the tree's title.

However, if two or more equal-ranking adjectives come before an adjective/noun phrase, then the equal-ranking adjectives should be separated by a comma.

> Her *new, blue* nylon collar still hung on a hook by the back door.

Adjectives are of equal rank if they can be switched in the sentence without changing the meaning of the sentence.

This works:

> The *tall, lanky* students play basketball.

This also works:

> The *lanky, tall* students play basketball.

Adjectives can modify
only nouns and pro-
nouns. Adjectives do not
modify other adjectives.

The adjectives in the following sentence are not of equal rank (and hence need no comma) because when we switch the adjectives, it changes the meaning of the sentence.

This works:

Several tall students play basketball.

This doesn't:

Tall several students play basketball.

PRACTICE 2-7

As practice, punctuate these sentences and then diagram them. You'll find the answers in the appendix.

1. My grandmother's musty old fur coat is in the attic.

2. The tall yellow fragrant flower is on display in the window.

3. The bouncer with cold piercing black eyes pointed to the door.

4. The fierce fragile tiger eats with her cubs.

5. The lively fun-loving hard-working singers practiced into the night.

Multiple Adverbs

This sentence illustrates that more than one adverb can modify one verb.

The ship **sailed** *swiftly* and *strongly* through the choppy seas.

Step 1:

Draw the horizontal and vertical baselines. Place the subject (ship) and the verb (**sailed**) in the respective locations, as you know well by now.

Now, here's what's new. Diagram the multiple adverbs (*swiftly* and *strongly*) by placing each adverb on its own diagonal line beneath the verb (**sailed**) in the order in which they occur in the sentence. Then, connect these multiple adverbs with a dotted line and the coordinating conjunction (and).

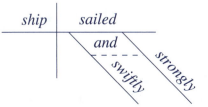

Step 2:

Now finish the diagram.

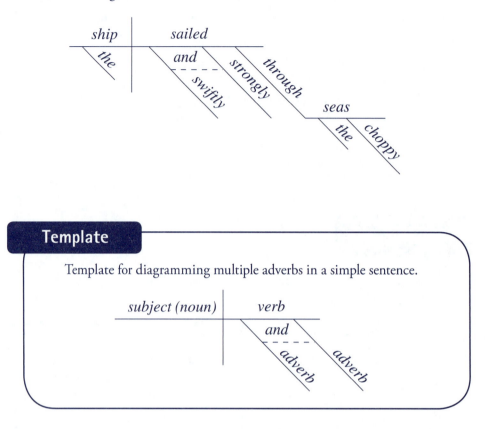

Template

Template for diagramming multiple adverbs in a simple sentence.

PRACTICE 2-8

Diagram these sentences containing multiple adverbs and check your work in the appendix.

1. The arrow flew straight and true into the heart of the dragon.

2. The marathoner ran winded and exhausted to the finish line.

3. The English students worked long and hard on their assignments.

4. Isaac spoke beautifully and passionately at the graduation ceremony.

5. The white water churned swiftly and dangerously over the rocks.

Adverbs That Modify Other Adverbs

This sentence illustrates that adverbs can modify other adverbs:

> I write *very **slowly***.

The word *slowly* is an adverb telling how I write. *Very* is an adverb telling how slowly I write; therefore, the adverb (*very*) modifies the adverb (***slowly***).

Step 1:

Draw the horizontal and vertical baselines, and place the subject and the verb on the subject and verb lines. Then, diagram the adverb (*slowly*) as modifying the verb (write).

Now here's what's new. Attach a diagonal line with a hook, as shown, beneath the line of the adverb (*slowly*), and place the adverb (very) on it to show that it modifies the adverb (*slowly*).

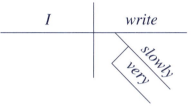

Template

Template for diagramming a compound adverb in a simple sentence.

subject (noun) | *verb*
    adverb
    adverb

PRACTICE 2–9

Practice diagramming these sentences containing adverbs modifying other adverbs. The answers are in the appendix.

1. The old man walked more quickly with his cane.

2. The car swerved too sharply.

3. The child jumped so high on the trampoline.

4. The trainer spoke extremely firmly.

5. The sports car turned very quickly.

Adverbs That Modify Adjectives

Sometimes adverbs, which traditionally modify verbs, can also modify adjectives and other adverbs. The following sentence is an example of an adverb that modifies an adjective:

Our **quite** *literal* interpretation worked.

The word *literal* is an adjective telling what kind of interpretation worked. The word **quite** is an adverb emphasizing the degree that the interpretation is literal; therefore, the adverb (**quite**) modifies the adjective (*literal*).

Step 1:

Draw the horizontal and vertical baselines, and place the subject and the verb on the subject and verb lines. Then, diagram the adjective (*literal*) on a diagonal line as modifying the subject (interpretation).

Now here's what's new. Attach a diagonal line with a hook, as shown, beneath the line of the adjective (*literal*), and place the adverb (**quite**) on it to show that it modifies the adjective (*literal*).

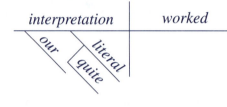

Template

Template for diagramming an adverb that modifies an adjective in a simple sentence.

PRACTICE 2-10

Practice diagramming these sentences containing adverbs modifying adjectives. The answers are in the appendix.

1. A very real danger for Robin Hood lived in the form of the Sheriff of Nottingham.

2. Her too subjective view of the world resulted in trouble.

3. The exceedingly dark clouds rained.

4. The roughly textured surface faded in the heat.

5. A terribly clever comedian laughed with the audience.

Diagramming Direct and Indirect Objects, and Subjective and Objective Complements

Nouns, pronouns, and adverbs can become parts of speech with special functions called direct and indirect objects, and objective and subjective complements. You'll learn to recognize these parts by where they are placed and how they are used in a sentence. However, before you can learn about objects and complements, you will need to know some basic facts about verbs.

Fast Facts About Verbs

Although you'll be learning in depth about verbs in Chapter 7, we are presenting a few specific facts about verbs and their complements now to help you understand, identify, and diagram direct objects.

What is a complement? The word complement is defined as "anything that completes the whole." A complement is a noun or adjective needed by a verb to complete a grammatical sentence.

Not all sentences require complements. For example, the following sentence is complete without a complement:

Terry **ran**.

However, many sentences need complements to complete their meaning, as in the following example:

Terry **gave** the book to me.

Complements fit into two main categories: (1) those that follow an **action verb**, and (2) those that follow a **linking verb**. To explain direct and indirect objects, we are focusing now on action verbs.

Complements that follow an **action verb** are called *objects*.

An **action verb** describes physical or mental action.

The student **read** the book.

The teacher **prepared** the exam.

The principal **ate** her breakfast.

Brenda **delivered** the morning papers.

I **believe** the news.

We **realize** his sincerity.

*A little grammar vocabulary to impress your friends: Not all verbs take direct objects. For example in the sentence, "The cow jumped over the moon," jumped is not followed by a direct object but is followed by a prepositional phrase. Verbs that are not followed by direct objects are called **intransitive verbs**. Verbs that are followed by direct objects are called **transitive verbs**. In other words, transitive verbs transfer action from one thing to another.*

Direct Object

Here is a sentence that contains an action verb followed by a direct object (*italic*).

My sister **plays** the *guitar*.

The word **plays** is the verb; sister is the subject of the sentence. But, what is *guitar*? Grammatically, it is a noun, but functionally it has a new meaning and a new name: direct object. What does *guitar* tell? It tells what my sister plays. Notice that it comes after the verb, but it does not explain or describe the subject.

He **loved** his *dog*.

What does *dog* tell? It tells whom "he" (the subject) loved. It does not explain or describe or complete the subject he.

You can find the *direct object* in the sentence by placing the word **whom** or **what** after the **action verb**. In short, the word that answers that question, and that does not explain or describe the subject, is the *direct object*.

A sentence can have two types of objects: direct and indirect. A direct object completes the action performed by the subject or asserted about the subject. It is the verb's target. You will learn about indirect objects later in this section.

Diagramming Direct Objects

Here's a sentence containing a direct object:

Bill **gave** the *ball* to Spot.

Step 1:

Diagram the subject and verb as you certainly know how to do well by now. Identify the direct object by noting that it follows an action verb and it answers the question "*What* did Bill give?"

Now here's what's new. Diagram the direct object by extending the horizontal baseline and then drawing a vertical line after the verb, as shown in the diagram below. (Do not extend the vertical line below the horizontal line.) Place the direct object on the extended baseline to the right of this new vertical line.

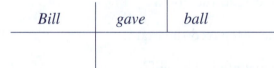

Step 2:

Now diagram the rest of the sentence. Notice that the preposition is placed under the verb because it tells *to whom* the ball was given.

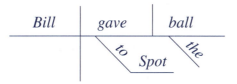

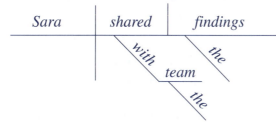

Identifying the direct object: Mentally place the word whom or what behind the action verb. The word in the sentence that answers that question is the direct object.

Here are some other examples:

Sara shared the findings with the team. (*What* did Sara share?)

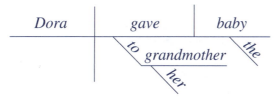

Dora gave the baby to her grandmother. (*Whom* did Dora give?)

PRACTICE 2–11

Now try diagramming these sentences containing direct objects. See the appendix for the answers.

1. The farmer planted the seeds in the field.

2. The cows ate the grass in the meadow.

3. The buyer studied the cows carefully.

4. Tim groomed his cow for the fair.

5. Tim's cow won a first-place ribbon.

Indirect Objects

Here's a sentence that contains a *direct object* and an **indirect object**.

> Bill gave **Brad** the *keys* to his car.

In this sentence, gave is the verb. Bill is the subject. Bill gave *what*? He gave *keys*, which is the *direct object*. But **to whom** did he give the keys? Ah! **Brad** is the indirect object.

Here's a trickier example:

> **Pass** *me* the *ball*.

In this sentence, pass is the verb. The word "you" (understood) is the subject. [You] pass *what* (ball) **to whom** (me)? So, *ball* is the direct object and **me** is the indirect object.

Notice a few things about these two sentences. Each contains a *direct object* and an **indirect object**. The *direct object* is identified by answering the question *whom* or *what* placed after the verb. The **indirect object** is identified by answering the question **to** or **for whom** the action was done. The words (**Brad** and **me**) do not answer the questions *whom* or *what* placed after the verb, but they do answer the question **to** or **for whom**. Also notice that there is no expressed preposition. A word that meets these requirements is an **indirect object**.

An **indirect object** names a person or other entity that is affected by the subject's action. For example,

> Bill gave Brad (indirect object) the keys (direct object).

Only certain transitive verbs such as ask, bring, buy, get, lend, offer, pay, promise, sell, show, tell, and write, take **indirect objects**.

Diagramming Indirect Objects

Here's a sentence containing an indirect object:

> Bill gave **Spot** the ball.

Step 1:

Diagram the subject, verb, and direct object as you have done before.

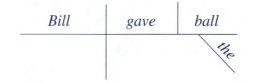

Step 2:

Identify the **indirect object** by noting that it follows an action verb, comes before the direct object, and answers the question "**Whom** did Bill give the ball to?"

Now, here's what's new. Diagram the ***indirect object*** by drawing a diagonal line that ends with a horizontal line (exactly like the prepositional phrase line) and place it underneath the verb. Then, write the indirect object on that line. The indirect object line in the diagram is always placed under the verb.

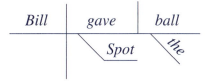

Here are some other sentences that contain ***indirect objects***:

Sara gave the team the findings. (*Whom* did Sara give the findings to?)

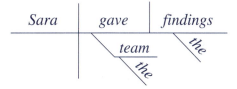

Tim told his cousins the story. (*Whom* did Tim tell?)

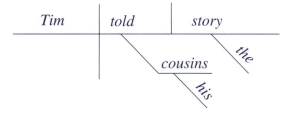

PRACTICE 2-12

Now try diagramming these sentences containing indirect objects. The answers are in the appendix.

1. The lead runner handed the second runner the baton.

2. The fans gave the entire team their support.

3. Terry left Pat the car keys under the welcome mat.

4. The principal handed the teaching assistant a book about classroom management.

5. Aurora fed her cat too many kitty treats.

Subjective Complements

The complements that follow "linking verbs" are called *subjective complements.*

More Fast Facts About Verbs

Only linking verbs can have subjective complements.

Linking verbs are a type of verb that connects or links the subject to its complement. Linking verbs describe the subject, but they do not perform any action. The verb **to be** is a linking verb. Forms of **to be** include **is, are, was, were, am, being,** and **been**.

> She **is** nice.
>
> The clouds **are** dark and gray.
>
> Tony **was** talented.
>
> They **were** writers.
>
> I **am** relaxed.
>
> The dog is **being** good.
>
> We have **been** to London.

Other linking verbs express sense perception such as sight, smell, taste, sound, and feel.

> The vet **looked** like a professional.
>
> The dog **smells** skunky.
>
> The strawberries **tasted** fresh.
>
> The child's cry **sounds** sad.
>
> The pillow **felt** soft.

Note that the same word can be a linking verb and an action verb, but the word has different meanings in these cases. For example,

> Linking verb: The actor **sounded** loud.
>
> Action verb: The actor **sounded** the opening act.

The linking verb **sounded** describes the actor—how she sounded. The actor in this case is not performing the action. The action verb **sounded** describes something the actor does.

The Subjective Complement Identity Test

A subjective complement is a word or group of words used after a linking verb that refers to and describes (completes) the subject. The subjective complement must do these four things to pass the identity test:

1. Answer the question **who** or **what** when placed after the verb.

2. Tell **who** or **what** the subject is.

3. Explain or describe or mean the same thing as the subject.

4. Follow a linking verb, such as **is, be, am, are, was, were, seem,** and **feel**.

For example,

> The student is a **member** of the band.

1. The word **member** answers the question of **who** or **what** when placed after the verb.

2. The word **member** tells **who** or **what** the subject is.

3. The words **member** and **student** mean the same person.

4. The word **member** follows the linking verb **is**.

The word **member** is therefore the subjective complement in the sentence.

A subjective complement can be a noun, an adjective, or a group of words that functions as a noun or adjective. However, it cannot be an adverb.

> The cat is **friendly**.

The word *friendly* is the subjective complement in this sentence because it meets the four criteria above. It follows a linking verb and the sentence is not complete without the subjective complement.

> She played **brilliantly**.

The word *brilliantly* is not a subjective complement. It follows an action verb, so it is an adverb. It tells **how** she played, not **what**.

Subjective Complement Types

There are two types of subjective complements: (1) a **predicate adjective**, and (2) a **predicate nominative**.

A **predicate adjective** is a descriptive adjective used after a linking verb. The following sentences contain predicate adjectives:

> The dog is **hungry**.

> The vet is **ready** for surgery.

> The owner was **nervous**.

Rule

As described in Lester (2001), to distinguish a predicate adjective from a verb, use the "very" test. If you can use the word "very" with the word following the verb, then that word is a predicate adjective. For example,

We were very running. (running is a verb)

The directions were very confusing. (confusing is a predicate adjective)

A **predicate nominative** is a noun or pronoun that identifies or renames the subject, and it is also used after a linking verb. The following sentences contain predicate nominatives:

Her favorite food is **pizza**.

The fish is **Flipper**.

The mountain is her **refuge**.

Diagramming Subjective Complements

Both types of subjective complements—predicate adjectives and predicate nominatives—are diagrammed in the same way. The two following example sentences contain subjective complements—the first is a predicate adjective (**bold**), and the second is a predicate nominative (***bold italic***).

My friends are **talented**.

My friends are my ***estate***. – Emily Dickinson

Step 1:

Diagram the subject and verb as you have already learned.

Step 2:

Identify the subjective complement in the sentence by noting that it follows a linking verb and refers back to the subject.

Now here's what's new. Place the subjective complement to the right of the verb on the same line, and separate it by drawing a backslash between the verb and subjective complement, as shown in the diagrams below:

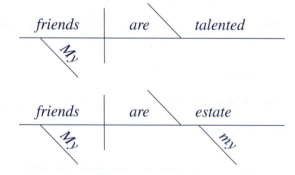

Here are more examples diagramming subjective complements,

The dreamers are the saviors of the world. – James Allen

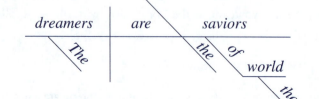

Happiness is a function of creativity. – Martin Grotjahn

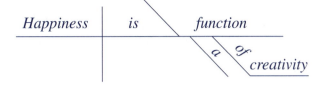

Rule

Here is a grammar rule you can understand by diagramming subjective complements. Verbs agree in number with their subjects and not with the subjective complement.

His problem is frequent headaches.

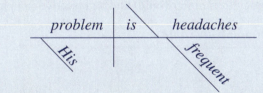

Frequent headaches are his problem.

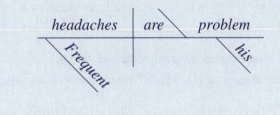

PRACTICE 2-13

Now try diagramming subjective complements for yourself. The answers are in the appendix.

1. "Imagination is the power of the mind over the possibility of things."
   – Wallace Steven

2. That film is a waste of time.

3. Her medical skill is obvious.

4. The students are quick learners.

5. The group of engineering students is talented at math.

Objective Complements

An objective complement is a noun or a descriptive adjective placed after a direct object that completes its meaning (refers back to, or means the same thing as, the direct object).

The newspaper named her the **winner**. (She is the winner.)

Objective complements usually follow the direct object and mean the same thing as the direct object (or refer to the direct object). Here is another example:

The students believed the movie a **hoax**. (The movie equals a hoax.)

In both of the examples above, the objective complements are nouns. The following is an example of an objective complement that is a descriptive adjective:

The critic called the book **contrived**.

Diagramming Objective Complements

This sentence contains a direct object (**bold**) and an objective complement (*italic*).

The team made **him** *captain*.

Step 1:

Diagram the subject, verb, and direct object as you have already learned.

Step 2:

Identify the objective complement in the sentence by noting that it follows a direct object and means the same thing or refers back to the direct object.

Here's what's new. Place the objective complement to the right of the direct object on the same horizontal line separated by a backslash, as shown in the diagram below:

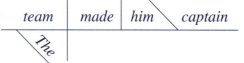

PRACTICE 2-14

Practice diagramming these sentences containing objective complements. Check your answers in the appendix.

1. The jury declared him innocent.

2. The projector makes the image clear.

3. Julie considered the fundraiser a success.

4. The Bishop crowned William King of England.

5. The doctor proclaimed the patient's progress a miracle.

Two Stragglers—Diagramming Appositives and Nouns of Address

An **appositive** is a noun or a pronoun that follows a noun or pronoun and explains or identifies it.

> My mother, the **principal**, is organizing the fundraising event.

An **appositive phrase** is an appositive with all its modifiers.

> My mother, the principal of the local elementary school, is organizing the fundraising event.

Diagramming Appositives

This sentence contains an appositive.

> The tournament champion, **Tiger Woods**, defended his title.

Step 1:

Diagram the parts of this sentence as you have already learned, leaving extra space on the subject line for the appositive.

Step 2:

Here's what's new. Write the appositive (**Tiger Woods**) on the subject line after the subject but before the vertical subject/verb divider line, and place it within parentheses, as shown in the diagram below. Finish the diagram as you know how.

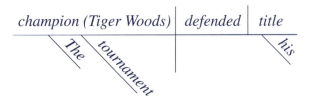

Diagramming Appositive Phrases

This is a sentence containing an appositive phrase.

> Her mother, **the principal of the local elementary school**, is a reading specialist.

Step 1:

Diagram the parts of this sentence as you have already learned, leaving space after the subject for the subject of the appositive phrase.

Step 2:

Write the appositive subject (**principal**) within parentheses on the subject line immediately after the subject it modifies (mother). Here's what's new. Diagram all the modifiers of the appositive under it as shown:

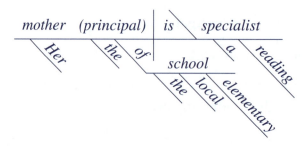

Rule

Appositives are usually set off with commas. However, if the appositive or appositive phrase is essential to the meaning of the sentence, commas should not be used to set off the appositive. For example,

The soccer player the one in the bleachers is the best player.

PRACTICE 2-15

Practice diagramming these sentences containing appositive phrases. Check your answers in the appendix.

1. The orthopedic surgeon, a knee specialist, replaced Dan's damaged knee.

2. Dan, a scientist at a laboratory, received six weeks of sick time for recovery.

3. The mice, a control group in Dan's research project, escaped from their cages.

4. Lisa, the janitor at the lab, caught the mice in a live trap.

5. Dan's research project, the impact of belching mice on the environment, missed an important deadline.

Nouns of Address

A noun of address is the name of the person being addressed in a sentence. It ***should be*** set off by commas. For example,

Tim, the books are in the box.

Diagramming Nouns of Address

This sentence contains a noun of address and a direct object.

Steve, take the dog for a walk.

Step 1:

Diagram the sentence as you have learned.

Step 2:

Here's what's new. Place the noun of address (Steve) on its own line above the diagram.

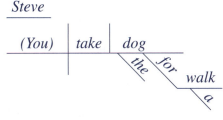

PRACTICE 2-16

1. The box is in the attic, Lori.

2. Pat, your home is beautiful.

3. Mabel, get your elbows off the table.

4. Splash, you are a good horse.

5. Open the door, George.

COMPREHENSIVE PRACTICE 2-17

Practice diagramming these sentences containing examples from each of the lessons within Chapter 2. Check your answers in the appendix.

1. The mayor gave the hero the key to the city.

2. Frank, tell Sara the news about the new house.

3. Red and yellow roses lined the path in the rose garden.

4. Jack and Jill traveled over the mountain and arrived at their grandmother's apartment.

5. Pam, a respected artist, taught the children at the camp her watercolor technique.

6. The horse ate the oats in the field and waited patiently for the cowboy.

7. The exhausted workers walked slowly down the dusty dirt road.

8. Five students and the teacher traveled by plane to Mexico for a language course.

9. *Knowledge is power.* –Sir Francis Bacon

10. Our black and white kitten fought the alley cat and lost the tip of her ear.

11. The vet carefully and skillfully bandaged the injury.

12. Nevian, my 1-year-old niece, sings songs to her kitten.

13. Fred, give Pat, the lead builder, the paperwork for the project.

14. The keys to the sports car are in the drawer.

15. The board elected his relative the new company president.

16. Dave and Debbie quickly assigned Don the responsibility for the reunion.

17. Don swiftly delegated his new responsibility to the new guy, Drew.

18. The rodeo bull broke the fence and escaped into the fairgrounds.

19. The swimmer handed the child a photo of the swim team.

20. It is a beautiful day.

Chapter 3

Constructing the Compound Sentence

A **compound sentence** contains two or more independent clauses (i.e., sentences) joined together with proper punctuation. For example,

> Samantha is my sister, and she is going on the trip with me.

As addressed in Chapter 2, an **independent clause**: (1) contains at least a subject and a predicate, and (2) is a complete thought.

Each independent clause in a compound sentence should be able to stand alone as a simple sentence.

> Samantha is my sister. She is going on the trip with me.

The compound sentence is properly joined by punctuation in three ways:

▶ **1. Use a semicolon.**

A semicolon can be used between closely related independent clauses. For example,

> Jill and Jack studied for the test; they reviewed the chapters and all their old tests.

> The test was difficult; it contained ten essay questions.

> The questions had no relation to previous tests; they related only to new material.

▶ **2. Use a comma and a coordinating conjunction.**

A coordinating conjunction connects grammatically equal elements, in the compound sentence, it connects two independent clauses. The coordinating conjunctions are

> and, but, or, nor, for, so, yet

Learning Objectives for Chapter 3

After studying this chapter, you will be able to

- Define and recognize a compound sentence
- Diagram and properly punctuate compound sentences
- Recognize and fix the punctuation problems of run-ons and comma splices

---

For example,

> We studied for the test, **and** we earned good grades.
>
> The dog bit the mailman, **but** the bite did not puncture the skin.
>
> I am hiking the trails in Montana, **or** I am fishing with friends in Alaska.

▶ **3. Use a conjunctive adverb preceded by a semicolon and followed by a comma.**

Conjunctive adverbs are adverbs used to indicate the relation between independent clauses.

A LIST OF COMMONLY USED CONJUNCTIVE ADVERBS			
accordingly	finally	likewise	specifically
also	furthermore	meanwhile	still
anyway	hence	moreover	subsequently
besides	however	nevertheless	then
certainly	incidentally	next	therefore
consequently	indeed	otherwise	thus
conversely	instead	similarly	

For example,

> The parade organizers planned for rain; **however**, they didn't plan for the snowstorm.
>
> The first floats in the parade became stuck in a foot of snow; **therefore**, the remaining floats and bands waited for hours in the procession.
>
> We will need to remove the furniture from the room before refinishing the hardwood floors; **otherwise**, the dust and wood particles will cover everything.

Rule

Punctuation for Compound Sentences

1. independent clause; independent clause.

2. independent clause; therefore, independent clause.

> however
> nevertheless
> consequently
> furthermore
> moreover, etc.

3. independent clause, and independent clause.

or
but
yet
so
nor
for

Diagramming Compound Sentences

Diagramming compound sentences is very similar to diagramming simple sentences except now you are working with more than one sentence. The following sections show you how to diagram the same compound sentence using each of the three ways to join independent clauses.

Diagramming a Compound Sentence Joined with a Semicolon

My friend is a mountain climber; she is fearless.

Step 1:

Diagram the two independent clauses, placing the first independent clause diagram above the second. Leave enough room between the two diagrams to connect them later.

First independent clause:

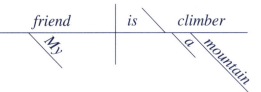

Second independent clause:

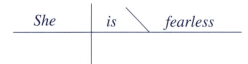

Step 2:

Now connect them by starting to draw a dotted vertical line from the verb in the first sentence down toward the verb in the second sentence. About half way down, draw a solid horizontal line, and then finish drawing the rest of the dotted vertical line to reach the verb of the second diagrammed sentence. Write the semicolon on the solid horizontal line.

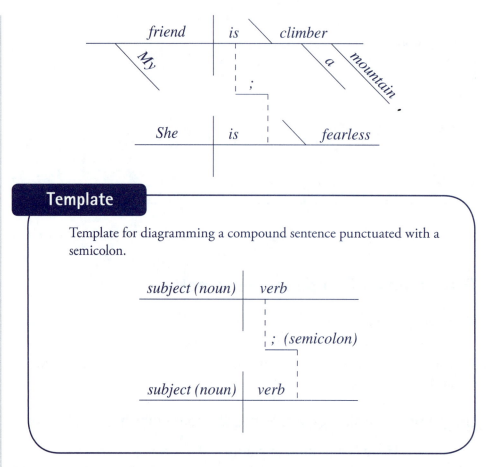

Template for diagramming a compound sentence punctuated with a semicolon.

subject (noun) | verb

; (semicolon)

subject (noun) | verb

Diagramming a Compound Sentence Joined with a Coordinating Conjunction

My friend is a mountain climber, and she is fearless.

Step 1:

Diagram the two independent clauses, placing the first independent clause diagram above the second.

First independent clause:

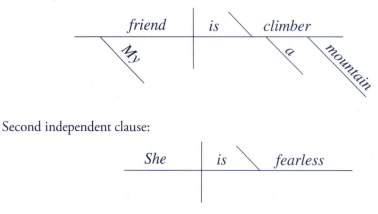

Second independent clause:

She | is \ fearless

Step 2:

Connect the independent clauses from verb to verb with a vertical dotted line, solid horizontal line, and dotted line, as you did before. The only difference between diagramming a compound sentence joined with a semicolon and doing one with a coordinating conjunction is that the conjunction as well as the punctuation is written on the solid horizontal line connecting the independent clauses, as shown:

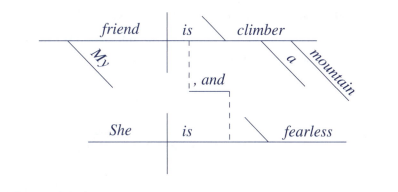

Template

Template for diagramming a compound sentence joined with a coordinating conjunction preceded by punctuation.

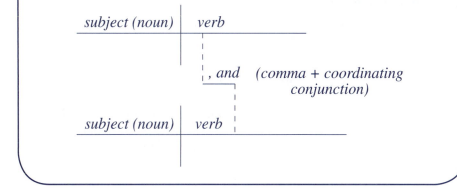

Diagramming a Compound Sentence Joined with a Conjunctive Adverb Preceded by a Semicolon and followed by a Comma

My friend is a mountain climber; moreover, she is fearless.

Step 1:

Diagram the two independent clauses, as you know how by now.

First independent clause:

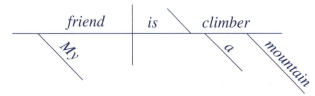

Second independent clause:

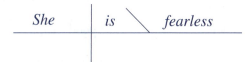

Step 2:

Connect the independent clauses from verb to verb with a vertical dotted line, solid horizontal line, and dotted line, as you did before. The only difference between diagramming a compound sentence joined with a semicolon and doing one with a conjunctive adverb is that the adverb as well as the punctuation is written on the solid horizontal line connecting the independent clauses, as shown:

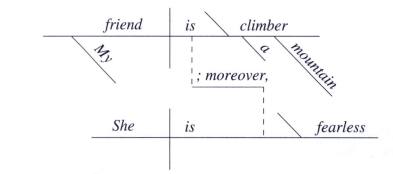

Template

Template for diagramming a compound sentence joined by a conjunctive adverb preceded by punctuation.

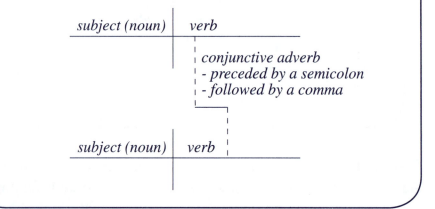

PRACTICE 3-1

Diagram each of the following sentences, and through the diagrams determine which sentences are simple and which are compound. See the appendix for the answers.

1. Sara and Jim studied many hours for the test and played into the weekend.

2. Sara and Jim studied many hours for the test, and they played into the weekend.

3. Jim is my brother; therefore, he understands our family.

4. Jim is my favorite brother and a good friend.

5. Jim studies many hours and plays many hours; he loves life.

The Run-on and the Comma Splice

When a compound sentence is not properly joined by punctuation (in one of the three ways you learned in the last section of this chapter), the result can be a "run-on sentence" or a "comma splice."

A **run-on** occurs when independent clauses (i.e., sentences) are joined with NO punctuation.

My friend is a mountain climber she is fearless.   (run-on)

A **comma splice** can occur when independent clauses are joined with ONLY a comma, which is not enough punctuation.

My friend is a mountain climber, she is fearless.   (comma splice)

To avoid these errors, you must be able to (1) identify the problem, and (2) insert the proper punctuation. Diagramming compound sentences can help you do that.

PRACTICE 3-2

Diagram each of the following incorrectly punctuated sentences. Identify the problem, and fix the run-on or comma splice in your diagram by making a compound sentence. The answers are provided in the appendix.

1. We went into the classroom with our books, we studied into the night.

2. We studied before the test we celebrated after the test.

3. The cat and the dog raced through the yard, they stopped at the fence.

4. The deadline for this year's applications passed it was last week.

   Now here's a challenge:

5. The fly fisherman stood on the bank of the sparkling river he selected the perfect fly and cast his line onto the rippling surface.

COMPREHENSIVE PRACTICE 3-3

Practice diagramming these sentences containing examples from each of the lessons within Chapter 3. Check your answers in the appendix. Note that some of these sentences contain a helping verb and a main verb. Please see the section on helping verbs in Chapter 7 if you do not understand how to diagram a helping verb with a main verb.

1. The knife is sharp; therefore, you do not run with it.

2. The students studied hard for the test on Friday, and they played during the weekend.

©2008 by Marye Hefty, Sallie Ortiz, Sara Nelson

3. The birds are flying home for the winter; they are flying over the frozen lake.

4. My computer at work is old; however, it runs the latest software.

5. The wealthy tourist will ski the mountains in Montana, or he will suntan on the beach in Hawaii.

6. The wealthy tourist will ski the mountains in Montana or suntan on the beach in Hawaii.

7. The door is locked, but they have a key.

8. The door is locked; moreover, it is bolted strongly.

9. I am finishing all of my homework; then, I will play the game.

10. The dedicated students answered the practice problems; hence, they could answer similar problems on the test.

11. The river water flows forcefully through the gorge, but it meanders through the flat land.

12. The cowboy and his horse searched for the lost sheep, and they found him under a willow tree.

13. The young man at the counter has the tickets, so you give him your money.

14. The inventor filed the patent; therefore, he owns the invention rights.

15. Ten inches of snow fell during the night; consequently, school closed for the day.

16. The team can prepare for the event, or the team can accept the consequences.

17. The team can prepare for the event or accept the consequences.

18. The very fine print states the important safety precautions, and she is farsighted without her glasses.

19. The message clearly stated the precautions, but she could not read them.

20. The test tube exploded; specifically, it shattered into a million pieces.

Building the Complex Sentence

A **complex sentence** contains an independent clause and at least one dependent clause.

> Samantha is a good student because she studies.

- An **independent clause** (also called the main clause of a complex sentence) contains a subject and a predicate (verb and any modifiers or complements) and expresses a complete thought. An independent clause is a complete sentence.

> Samantha is a good student.

Learning Objectives for Chapter 4

After studying this chapter, you will be able to

- Define and recognize a complex sentence
- Define, recognize, and diagram the three types of dependent clauses: adjective, adverb, and noun
- Know how to correctly use who and whom
- Know how to properly punctuate adverb clauses

- A **dependent clause** (also called a subordinate clause) contains a subject and a predicate as well, but does not express a complete thought by itself. A dependent clause must be somehow connected to an independent clause to form a complete sentence.

> *Because she studies*, Samantha is a good student.

> Samantha is a good student *because she studies*.

Three Types of Dependent Clauses

There are three types of dependent clauses: (1) adjective clauses, (2) adverb clauses, and (3) noun clauses. As the names imply, these three types are used in sentences as specific parts of speech (either as an adjective, adverb, or noun).

An adjective clause functions as an adjective to modify or describe a noun or a pronoun by answering questions such as Which one? How many? and What kind?

An adverb clause functions as an adverb to modify a verb, an adjective, or another adverb. (It usually answers one of the questions: When? Where? How? Why? or To what degree?)

A **noun clause** functions as a noun as a subject, direct object, object of the preposition, or subjective complement.

If you are feeling a little dizzy with details, don't worry. The next subsections will help you identify the clause types and diagram complex sentences.

The Adjective Clause

A noun or a pronoun can be modified by an adjective that is a single word (blue house), a phrase (the house in my neighborhood), or a dependent clause (the house, which is blue).

An adjective clause contains a subject and a verb and functions as an adjective (as a unit to modify a noun or a pronoun). An adjective clause is a dependent clause.

Adjective clauses are usually introduced by pronouns. The following examples of adjective clauses (*in italics*) show the pronouns in bold.

The most common of these pronouns are called relative pronouns. They "relate" back to the antecedent, which is the noun to their immediate left. (See the definition of antecedent below.) The relative pronouns are who, whom, whose, which, or that. Because these relative pronouns are often at the beginning of adjective clauses, these adjective clauses are also called "relative clauses."

Some other pronouns that can start an adjective clause are whoever, whomever, whichever, what, whenever, and why.

> The dog ***that*** *jumps my fence* has big floppy ears.
>
> The dog fetches tennis balls from his owner ***whom*** *the dog adores.*
>
> The tennis balls, ***which*** *sometimes fly over my fence*, are chewed and soiled.
>
> They are used tennis balls ***that*** *the dog chases.*
>
> This owner is a dog lover ***whose*** *work with dogs never stops.*
>
> The dog just jumped over my fence ***where*** *the gate is closed.*

The Antecedent—a Grammar Word That Is Important to Know

The word that a relative pronoun refers to is called an antecedent.

For the relative pronoun *who* in the sentence—The dog owner, who walks that dog with floppy ears, is my brother—the antecedent is owner (i.e., the word who refers back to).

For the relative pronoun *whom* in the sentence—The dog fetches tennis balls from his owner whom the dog adores—the antecedent is owner.

For the relative pronoun *which* in the sentence—The tennis balls, which sometimes fly over my fence, are chewed and soiled—the antecedent is balls.

For the relative pronoun *that* in the sentence—They are used tennis balls that the dog chases—the antecedent is balls.

Note in all the examples above that the antecedent is the word that immediately precedes the relative pronoun.

Rule

Who, whom, and *whose* are used when referring back to people. (Stated in a more technical way: *Who, whom*, and *whose* have antecedents that are people.)

That and *which* are used when referring back to objects, animals, or ideas. (That and *which* have antecedents that are objects, animals, or ideas.)

Where is used to refer back to nouns of location. (*Where* has antecedents that are locations.)

How to Identify an Adjective Clause

Here are the clues to identifying an adjective clause:

1. It functions as an adjective, answering the questions: Which one? or What kind?

2. It contains a subject and a verb (which are essential for a clause).

3. It follows the noun that it modifies (the antecedent).

4. It usually begins with a relative pronoun (which refers to the antecedent in the independent, or joined, clause).

Special Functions of Relative Pronouns in an Adjective Clause

Before you begin diagramming an adjective clause, here are a few more facts you will need to know about the relative pronouns (who, whom, whose, which, or that).

Relative pronouns function within the adjective clause either as an adjective, subject, direct object, or object of a preposition. (See Chapter 5—Pronouns—for diagrams that clearly show these functions.)

Relative pronoun as an adjective:

> My youngest son, *whose friend owns a car*, is driving him to school.

In the dependent clause *whose friend owns a car*, "whose" is acting as an adjective.

Relative pronoun as a subject:

> The car *that is speeding down the street* is red.

In the dependent clause *that is speeding down the street*, "that" functions as a subject.

Relative pronoun as a direct object:

> The coat *that you forgot* is in the hall closet.

In the dependent clause *that you forgot*, "that" is acting as the direct object of "you forgot."

Relative pronoun as the object of a preposition:

> The teacher of *whom you spoke* is my mentor.

The dependent clause *whom you spoke* is the object of the preposition "of."

Relative pronouns omitted:

Sometimes in a sentence the relative pronoun is omitted because it is understood, but this understood pronoun still serves its usual functions. For example:

> *The tickets I needed were sold out.*

> The tickets [that] I needed were sold out.

How to Diagram an Adjective Clause

These are the basic steps for diagramming a sentence containing an adjective clause. This section includes specific examples of diagrams of each of the special functions of pronouns within an adjective clause.

1. Diagram the independent clause first. Below it will go the dependent adjective clause.

2. Diagram the relative pronoun within the dependent clause according to its grammatical function. For example, place relative pronouns that function as objects of prepositions within the part of the diagram for the prepositional phrase. Place relative pronouns that function as direct objects in the object position to the right of the verb. (This means moving the relative pronoun from the beginning of the relative clause to its appropriate place of function within the sentence diagram.)

3. For omitted relative pronouns, add the "omitted but understood" relative pronouns in parentheses in the appropriate place on the diagram.

4. Using a dotted line, connect the pronoun in the dependent clause to the noun it modifies in the independent clause.

Diagramming an Adjective Clause with a Relative Pronoun that Functions as a Subject

She spoke with a student *who* lives in Fiji.

Step 1:

Identify the independent clause. Diagram the independent clause.

Step 2:

Identify the dependent clause. Diagram the dependent clause below the diagram for the independent clause. Using a dotted line, connect the pronoun in the dependent clause to the noun it modifies in the independent clause.

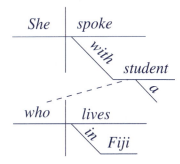

PRACTICE 4-1

See if you can diagram these sentences with relative pronouns that function as subjects. The answers are in the appendix.

1. The pitcher, who arrived from the minor leagues, pitched a no hitter.

2. The house, which is brick, is a historic landmark.

3. The bird that is yellow is my bird.

Diagramming an Adjective Clause with a Relative Pronoun that Functions as a Direct Object

She spoke with a student whom you know.

Step 1:

Identify the independent clause. Diagram the independent clause.

Step 2:

Identify the dependent clause. Diagram the dependent clause below the diagram for the independent clause. Using a dotted line, connect the pronoun in the dependent clause to the noun it modifies in the independent clause. (See the next page.)

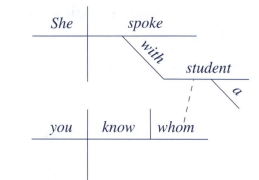

PRACTICE 4-2

Now diagram these sentences with relative pronouns that function as direct objects. The answers are in the appendix.

1. The children ate the cotton candy that they bought at the fair.

2. We grilled the trout that we caught in the lake.

3. We stayed with the people whom you suggested.

Diagramming an Adjective Clause with a Relative Pronoun that Functions as an Adjective

She spoke with a student *whose* stories are vivid.

Step 1:

Identify the independent clause. Diagram the independent clause.

Step 2:

Identify the dependent clause. Diagram the dependent clause below the diagram for the independent clause. Using a dotted line, connect the pronoun in the dependent clause to the noun it modifies in the independent clause.

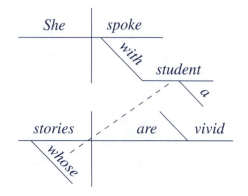

PRACTICE 4-3

Try your hand at diagramming these sentences with relative pronouns that function as adjectives. The answers are in the appendix.

1. The person whose cell phone rang during the play is thoughtless.

2. The waitress, whose name is Cindy, took our order.

3. The parent whose child is in my son's class spoke about the proposed program.

Diagramming an Adjective Clause with a Relative Pronoun that Functions as an Object of a Preposition

Both of these sentences are diagrammed in the same way.

> She studied the natives about whom the anthropologist spoke.

> She studied the natives the anthropologist spoke about.

Step 1:

Identify the independent clause. Diagram the independent clause.

Step 2:

Identify the dependent clause. Diagram the dependent clause below the diagram for the independent clause. Using a dotted line, connect the pronoun in the dependent clause to the noun that it modifies in the independent clause.

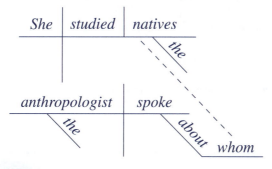

PRACTICE 4-4

Now try diagramming these sentences with a relative pronoun that functions as an object of a preposition. The answers are in the appendix.

1. The lawyer reviewed the facts on which the case depended.

2. The librarian gave the author about whom she raved a rare book.

3. The river guide gave the oars to his partner for whom the river got its name.

Diagramming an Adjective Clause with an Omitted but Understood Relative Pronoun

She knew the language [that] I studied once.

Step 1:

Identify the independent clause. Diagram the independent clause.

Step 2:

Identify the dependent clause. Diagram the dependent clause below the diagram for the independent clause. Using a dotted line, connect the pronoun in the dependent clause to the noun that it modifies in the independent clause.

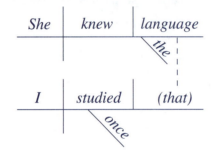

PRACTICE 4–5

These sentences contain an omitted but understood relative pronoun for you to practice diagramming. The answers are in the appendix.

1. The music they enjoyed filled their hearts.

2. The dance they learned was beautiful.

3. The discovery the scientific team made in December saved a life in March.

Rule

Understanding When to Use Who or Whom

It is only in relative pronouns that who changes form. (As stated previously, the relative pronouns *who, whose, whom, which,* and *that* attach adjective clauses to their antecedent—the noun or pronoun modified.)

Who, a subjective case pronoun, can be used only for subjects and subjective complements.

Whom, an objective case pronoun, can be used only for objects.

Here are the rules:

1. Use *who* or *whoever* when the pronoun is the subject of the verb.

   Whoever is knocking at the door?

   I question *who* wrote these directions.

2. Use *who* or *whoever* when the pronoun is the subjective complement.

   The masked rider was *who*?

   No one knew who the masked rider was.

3. Use *whom* or *whomever* when the pronoun is the direct object of a verb or the object of a preposition.

   Whom did he select?

   He can select *whomever* he wants.

   With *whom* were you talking?

4. At the beginning of *who/whom* questions, use *who* if the question is about the subject or *whom* if the question is about the object.

Practice with *Who* and *Whom*

1. From (who, whom) did you get those flowers?

2. (Who, Whom) is your friend?

3. The company selected (who, whom) for the honor?

4. (Who, Whom) knows how to use this new VCR?

5. No one knew (who, whom) gave us the flowers.

6. A tough one: Give this work to (whoever, whomever) looks bored.

Answers:

1. Whom (object of the preposition "from")

2. Who (subject of the verb)

3. Who (subject of the verb)

4. Who (subject of the verb)

5. Who (subjective complement)

6. Whoever because this is the subject of looks bored; the object of the preposition to is the entire clause whoever looks bored.

Practice your new skill by diagramming the following sentences containing adjective clauses. The answers are in the appendix.

1. My parents own a llama that I adore.

2. The llama, whose name is Fred, spits at most people.

3. Fred is a llama that spits at most people.

4. Fred is a llama that my parents own.

5. Fred sleeps under the apple tree we planted for shade.

The Adverb Clause

An adverb clause is a dependent clause that modifies a verb, adjective, or other adverb. Like an adverb, an adverb clause answers the questions: Where? Why? When? To what extent? Under what condition? In what manner?

An adverb clause begins with a subordinating conjunction, which shows a logical relationship between the adverb clause and the independent clause. Some common subordinating conjunctions are shown below:

Relationship Used for Expressing the following:	Subordinating Conjunction
Cause	because, as, since
Comparison	as, as if, as though, than
Condition	unless, if, even if
Contrast	though, while, although, even though, whereas
Place	where, wherever
Purpose	that, so that
Result	so
Time	until, till, before, when, whenever, after, once, while, as long as, as soon as

A clue to identifying adverb clauses is to know that these clauses are structurally very different from adjective clauses. In the adjective clause, the clue is the relative pronoun that begins the clause. This relative pronoun, as illustrated in the previous section, is an essential part of the dependent clause. It functions as a subject, object, or other part of speech within the sentence.

In the adverb clause, the subordinating conjunction is a conjunction—a connecting word. It is an introductory word that is not an essential part of speech within the dependent clause it introduces. The subordinating conjunction simply ties the dependent clause to the dependent clause. Here's an example,

We studied for the test **because** *we needed to pass the class.*

The subordinate conjunction **because** introduces the dependent clause **because** *we needed to pass the class.* This is an adverb clause because it modifies the verb telling *why* they studied.

How to Identify an Adverb Clause

Here are the clues to identifying an adverb clause:

1. It functions as an adverb, answering the questions *where, when, how, why, to what extent,* or *under what condition.*

2. It contains a subject and a verb in a dependent clause.

3. It begins with a subordinating conjunction.

How to Diagram an Adverb Clause

These are the basic steps for diagramming a sentence containing an adverb clause.

1. Identify and diagram the independent clause first.

2. Identify and diagram the adverb clause below the independent clause (excluding the subordinate conjunction).

3. Draw a dotted line from the verb in the dependent clause to the word modified in the independent clause.

4. Write the subordinating conjunction on the dotted line.

Essential words of an adverb clause may be omitted if no misunderstanding will occur. Such a clause is called an *elliptical clause.* Here is an example,

Terri can sing better than I (can sing).

Diagramming an Adverb Clause that Modifies a Verb

We found a rare book about the Titanic when we cleaned grandmother's attic.

Step 1:

Identify the independent clause. Diagram the independent clause.

Step 2:

Identify the dependent clause. Diagram the dependent clause below the diagram for the independent clause. Use a dotted line to connect the verb in the dependent clause to the word modified in the independent clause. Write the subordinating conjunction on the dotted line.

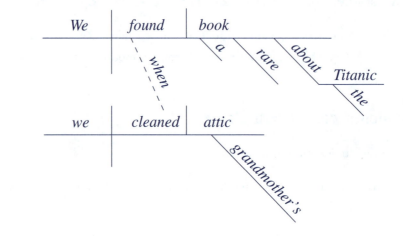

You can easily identify an adverb clause that modifies a verb because the dependent clause can be moved from the back of the sentence to the front of the sentence with the meaning still intact.

PRACTICE 4-7

Here are some practice sentences containing adverb clauses that modify verbs. The answers are in the appendix.

1. Because we practiced, we won the game.

2. The freshman had a party when the school year finished.

3. Although they loved school, they loved vacation too.

Diagramming an Adverb Clause that Modifies an Adjective

Adverbs can modify only predicate adjectives (i.e., a type of subjective complement) and cannot modify the modifying adjectives. Only two words can introduce an adverb clause that modifies an adjective: *that* and *than*. Some example sentences are provided below, and note that having "that" in parentheses indicates this word can be omitted in the sentence.

> We were positive (that) the car stopped.

> The traffic investigator was sure (that) the car ran the light.

> The car is more damaged than you think.

Let's diagram the following sentence:

> We were positive that the car stopped.

Step 1:

Identify the independent clause. Diagram the independent clause.

Step 2:

Identify the dependent clause. Diagram the dependent clause below the diagram for the independent clause. Use a dotted line to connect the verb in the dependent clause to the word modified in the independent clause. Write the subordinating conjunction on the dotted line.

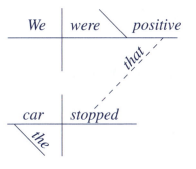

Rule

The word "that" is the only word that can be omitted as a subordinating conjunction in an adverb clause. All other subordinating conjunctions must be visible in the sentence.

Now, let's practice one more sentence with the word "that" omitted.

He felt certain the answer was correct.

Step 1:

Identify the independent clause. Diagram the independent clause.

Step 2:

Identify the dependent clause. Diagram the dependent clause below the diagram for the independent clause. Use a dotted line to connect the verb in the dependent clause to the word modified in the independent clause. Write the implied subordinating conjunction on the dotted line and place it in parentheses.

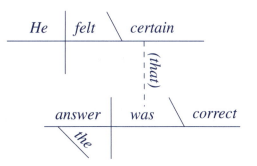

Here are some practice sentences containing adverb clauses that modify adjectives. The answers are in the appendix.

1. The family felt sad that the exchange student returned to his country.

2. They are sorry that the package arrived late.

3. The doctor is sure the virus is contained.

Diagramming an Adverb Clause that Modifies an Adverb

Than is the only subordinating conjunction that can be used as the connecting word when an adverb clause modifies an adverb. Adverb clauses modify comparative adverbs (which are formed using *–er* or *more*). Here are some examples of comparative adverbs.

> We rode *more quickly* than I liked.

> The red car sped *faster* than your car drove.

Let's practice diagramming this sentence:

> She climbed the mountain faster than the others climbed.

Step 1:

Identify the independent clause. Diagram the independent clause.

Step 2:

Identify the dependent clause. Diagram the dependent clause below the diagram for the independent clause. Use a dotted line to connect the verb in the dependent clause to the word modified in the independent clause. Write the subordinating conjunction on the dotted line.

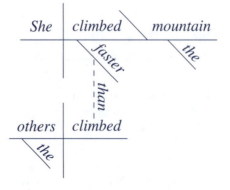

These practice sentences contain adverb clauses that modify adverbs. The answers are in the appendix.

1. Our hockey team finished the season better than the team from Troutdale finished.

2. The New York version of the play earned more than the producers expected.

3. The piano fell harder down the steps than the movers imagined.

Rule

Punctuation Rules for Adverb Clauses

As shown in the punctuation rules below, adverb dependent clauses that start a complex sentence contain a comma before the independent clause (separating the dependent from the independent clause).

Adverb clauses that end a complex sentence usually contain no comma. However, when the adverb clause begins with *although, even though*, or *though* (words indicating something contrary to expectations), then a comma is included after the independent clause and before the dependent clause.

#1 <u>dependent clause</u>, <u>independent clause</u>

    because

     since

     when

     while

    although

     after

#2 <u>independent clause</u> if <u>dependent clause</u>

          because

           since

           when

           while

           after

        even though

Sentence Fragments: A Problem You Can Identify and Solve

A dependent clause that is not connected to an independent clause is not a complete sentence—it is a sentence fragment. The following sentence fragments are dependent clauses that are not connected to independent clauses.

> When we go to the store.
>
> Because they shared around the campfire.
>
> If we go fishing.
>
> After all the boxes have been packed.

To become complete complex sentences, these dependent clauses need to be connected to independent clauses as shown:

> We can pick up the movie *when we go to the store*.
>
> > [independent clause + *dependent clause* = complex sentence]
>
> *When we go to the store*, we can pick up the movie.
>
> > [*dependent clause* + independent clause = complex sentence]
>
> They all knew the stories *because they shared them around the campfire*.
>
> > [independent clause + *dependent clause* = complex sentence]
>
> *If we go fishing*, we should take the boat.
>
> > [*dependent clause* + independent clause = complex sentence]
>
> We should take the boat *if we go fishing*.
>
> > [independent clause + *dependent clause* = complex sentence]
>
> *After all the boxes have been packed*, we should load the moving van.
>
> > [*dependent clause* + independent clause = complex sentence]
>
> We should load the moving van *after all the boxes have been packed*.
>
> > [independent clause + *dependent clause* = complex sentence]

When the dependent clause begins a sentence, it is separated from the independent clause with a comma (as shown in this sentence). When the dependent clause ends a sentence (follows the independent clause), it usually is not separated by a comma.

PRACTICE 4-10

Practice your skills at diagramming these sentences containing the adverb clauses you studied in this section. The answers are in the appendix.

1. Although we had no money, we were happy.

2. He sang in the shower when nobody was in the house.

3. The broken piano cost more than the movers thought.

4. The wildflowers in the field are more beautiful than the ones bought at the store.

5. Because it rained, the flowers bloomed.

The Noun Clause

A noun clause is a dependent clause that functions as a noun. Remember that a noun usually can be used as a subject, direct object, object of the preposition, and subjective complement. In the noun clause, this entire dependent clause is used as some function of a noun—an essential part of the sentence and not a modifier like the adjective and adverb clauses. The following example sentences illustrate this:

Noun clause as subject:

> *Whether we go today or tomorrow* is not important.

Noun clause as direct object:

> She believed (that) *Tim had the paperwork.*

Noun clause as the object of the preposition:

> They knew nothing about *where the paperwork was located.*

Noun clause as subjective complement:

> The rule is *that new employees have a physical.*

How to Identify a Noun Clause

Noun clauses are singular in number as illustrated in this sentence:

> *That the **dogs** all bark at **cars*** upsets the owner.

Notice how the entire noun clause is treated as a singular subject (although it contains plural nouns) and that this singular subject appropriately agrees in number with the singular verb.

Because noun clauses are always singular in number, the "it test" as described in Lester (2001) can be used to identify noun clauses.

Here's the "it test" for noun clauses: If "it" can clearly replace the dependent clause, then the clause is a noun clause.

Noun clause as subject:

> *Whether we go today or tomorrow* is not important.

> [It] is not important.

Noun clause as direct object:

> She believed (that) *Tim had the paperwork.*

> She believed [it].

Noun clause as the object of the preposition:

> They knew nothing about *where the paperwork was located.*

> They knew nothing about [it].

Noun clause as subjective complement:

The rule is *that new employees have a physical.*

The rule is [it].

If you can't decide if "that" in a sentence introduces a noun clause or an adjective clause, then use the *which test*, also described in Lester (2001).

If *which* cannot replace *that* at the beginning of a dependent clause, then it is a noun clause, as shown here:

Noun clause: The mother heard *that* her sons had a party.

Which test: The mother heard *which* her sons had a party.

If *which* can replace *that* at the beginning of a dependent clause, then *that* signals an adjective clause, as shown here:

Adjective clause: He has a plan *that* the council should approve.

Which test: He has a plan, *which* the council should approve.

Distinguishing between Two Types of Noun Clauses

Before you begin diagramming noun clauses, it is important to know one more thing. Noun clauses are put together with two structures. One type begins with the words *that, if,* or *whether (or not)*. This type is structured like an adverb clause because the dependent clause starts with a signal word that is not essential to the meaning of the sentence. Here are some examples,

We know ***that*** the river is deep.
Whether or not the river is deep makes no difference.
I don't know ***if*** the water is deep.

The other type contains an introductory word (usually beginning with wh-) that functions as a noun, adjective, or adverb.

Nouns: who, whoever, what, whatever, whom, whomever
Adjectives: which, whichever, whose
Adverbs: why, where, wherever, when, whenever, how, however

Here are some example sentences,

Whoever *crosses the river* gets to the other side. (Functions as a subject)
When *you swim* depends on the weather. (Functions as an adverb)

How to Diagram a Noun Clause

A complex sentence containing a noun clause is diagrammed differently from adjective and adverb clauses because the noun clause is usually an essential part of the sentence and not a modifier like the adjective and adverbial clause.

These are the basic steps for diagramming a sentence containing a noun clause.

1. Identify the dependent (noun) clause and its function within the complex sentence.

2. Diagram the dependent (noun) clause in its appropriate function place on stilts connected to the main sentence line.

3. Diagram the signal words that have no function within the sentence (*that, if, whether,* or *whether or not*) above the noun clause on a horizontal line that is connected to the noun clause with a dotted line.

4. Diagram the signal words that function as a part of speech in the sentence in the appropriate place (based on its function) within the dependent clause.

In the diagram instructions below, instead of accompanying written instructions, two diagrams are provided within each category below: one shows how to diagram a noun clause with a signal word that is not part of the meaning of the sentence, and one shows how to diagram a noun clause with a signal word that functions as part of the meaning of the sentence.

Diagramming Noun Clauses that Function as Subjects

Whether or not the river is deep makes no difference.

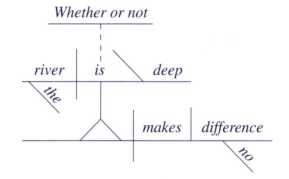

Whoever finishes the class earns a grade.

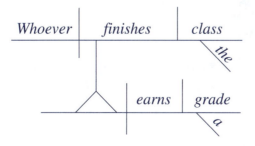

Practice diagramming these sentences containing noun clauses that function as subjects. The answers are in the appendix.

1. That the Steinway piano shattered into many pieces caused an uproar in the family.

2. Whether or not insurance covers the damage is an important question.

3. What the movers did to the piano concerned the corporate office.

Diagramming Noun Clauses that Function as Direct Objects

Santa Claus knows *the children are good.* (*That* is understood.)

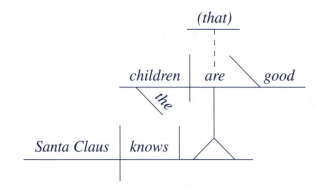

The parents really know what they are.

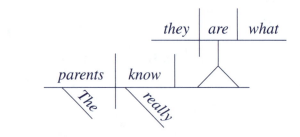

PRACTICE 4-12

Diagram the following sentences containing noun clauses that function as direct objects. The answers are in the appendix.

1. The rancher saved whatever lumber was in the barn.

2. He knew that the old lumber was valuable.

3. He believed it contained an undiscovered value.

Diagramming Noun Clauses that Function as the Object of the Preposition

The invitation said no words *about whether guests received a free dinner.*

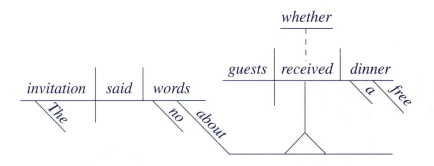

The children made lists *about whichever toys they wanted.*

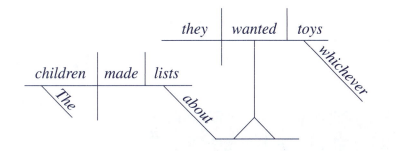

PRACTICE 4-13

Practice diagramming these sentences containing noun clauses that function as objects of prepositions. The answers are in the appendix.

1. The leader gave supplies for whatever situation was confronted.

2. I heard about what you said.

3. They gave thanks for what they had.

Diagramming Noun Clauses that Function as Subjective Complements

It appears *that she has the talent.*

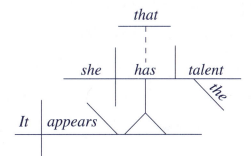

Talent is *what she has.*

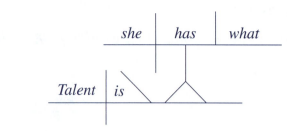

PRACTICE 4-14

Practice diagramming these sentences containing noun clauses that function as subjective complements. The answers are in the appendix.

1. The prize is whatever Don wants.

2. The problem is what the doctor thought.

3. The solution is whatever reduces the fever.

COMPREHENSIVE PRACTICE 4-15

Practice diagramming these sentences containing examples from each of the lessons in Chapter 4. Check your answers in the appendix.

1. Whoever broke the piano will pay for it.

2. The farmer who operates the neighborhood vegetable stand sells blueberries.

3. Whether or not we approve has little impact on her decision.

4. When we flipped the switch, light filled the room.

5. The piano weighed more than the movers expected.

6. He knows that you studied hard.

7. The famous monument, which is marble, survived the earthquake.

8. Brian recovered whatever books remained.

9. Because we wore rain gear, we stayed dry.

10. The car that is in the garage needs an oil change.

11. The volcano they climbed in the spring erupted in the summer.

12. Wind for the sail is what they need.

13. Our creek flooded because the unusually hot spring melted the snow.

14. Although we love school, we love vacation more.

15. The manager interviewed the recruit whom his employees selected.

16. The current is stronger than it appears from the shore.

17. The anonymous donor whose donation paid for the new building is generous.

18. Our canoe raced faster than the other canoes in the competition raced.

19. What you know about genealogy is impressive because you found information about my lost great-grandmother.

20. They knew that the solution was in the ancient riddle.

Chapter 5

Pronouns

A **pronoun** is a word that takes the place of a noun or another pronoun. The word the pronoun substitutes for is called the **antecedent**.

The horse galloped across the field, but *he* stopped at the river's edge.

(*He* substitutes for *horse*. *Horse* is the antecedent of *he*.)

The most commonly used pronoun is the personal pronoun.

> ## Learning Objectives for Chapter 5
>
> After studying this chapter, you will be able to
>
> - Define, recognize, and diagram the following pronoun types: personal, possessive, reflexive, intensive, indefinite, demonstrative, relative, interrogative, and reciprocal
> - Recognize and solve pronoun errors by applying diagramming skills

Personal Pronouns

The **personal pronoun** substitutes for persons and things.

- Some personal pronouns refer to the speaker (First Person).

    "*I* am talented," announced Bill.

    "Show *me* the proof," said Sam.

    "Give *us* the data," demanded the scientists.

    "*We* will believe what *we* can prove," proclaimed the assistants.

    "*My* proof is in the formula, and it is *mine*," stated Bill.

    "No, it is *our* formula," reminded Sam.

    "Okay, it is *ours*," said Bill.

- Some personal pronouns refer to the person spoken to (Second Person). For example

    "*You* are right," said Sam.

    "*Your* judgment is impeccable," replied Bill.

    "Yes, so is *yours*," stated Sam.

- Some personal pronouns refer to the person spoken about (Third Person).

> Bill did have talent. *He* understood ancient bugs better than Sam.
>
> Of course, Sara had talent too. *She* studied very ancient bugs.
>
> *It* was more than a hobby. *She* loved bugs. *They* fascinated *her*.
>
> Bill marveled at how *they* fascinated *her* more than *they* fascinated *him*.
>
> *Hers* was a true talent. *His* was a job.
>
> *Their* paths crossed because of a common interest.
>
> *Theirs* were lives devoted to science. *They* found meaning in *its* structure.
>
> Okay . . . the authors will stick to writing grammar books!

As shown above, personal pronouns change form depending on

1. who is speaking (referred to formally as "person"), including the gender of who is speaking

2. whether the pronoun is singular or plural (referred to as "number")

3. whether the pronoun is being used as a subject or subjective complement (subjective case), an object (objective case), or a possessive form.

The following tables show these personal pronoun changes relative to person, gender, number, and case:

Singular			
Person	Subject	Object	Possessive
First	I	me	my, mine
Second	you	you	your, yours
Third	he, she, it	him, her, it	his, hers, its

Plural		
Subject	Object	Possessive
we	us	our, ours
you	you	your, yours
they	them	their, theirs

How to Use Your Diagramming Skills to Solve Personal Pronoun Problems

Subjective Case Pronouns

As shown in the table on page 70, personal pronouns that are used as the subjects of sentences must use subjective case pronouns (also known as nominative case pronouns). The following pronouns can be easily memorized because they include a finite number:

- I

- he

- she

- we

- they

- you

- it

When you have memorized the above list, you will be able to use diagramming to quickly determine the correct pronoun.

Gina and [he, him] discussed the problem.

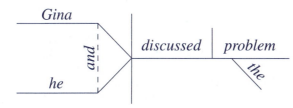

He and [her, she] watched the game.

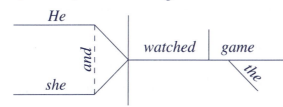

You and [us, we] should take the class.

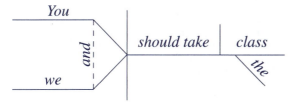

If you are unsure of what pronoun to use in compound pronoun situations, mentally eliminate one of the pronouns, and this will help you identify the correct pronoun.

He and [her, she] watched the game.

He watched the game.

She watched the game.

Rule

Pronouns may be used as appositives or in appositive phrases. A pronoun appositive must be in the same case as its antecedent, as shown below:

The painters, Thomas and she, painted the mural.

(not *her* because painters is a subject)

We the people refers to all people. (It is not "*us* the people" because we is a subject.)

PRACTICE 5-1

Diagram the following sentences to determine the correct personal pronoun. Again, say each pronoun separately to help you decide. The answers are in the appendix.

1. [He, Him] and [me, I] aced the test about pronouns.

2. Carol and [she, her] studied for hours.

3. My friends, Matt and [he, him], are hard workers.

4. [You, Your] and [they, them] need the money.

5. Tom and [he, him] discussed a solution.

"Woe is me."

The exception.

The English language is changing, and one example is the statement: Woe is me. To be grammatically correct, this should say, "Woe is I." However, "woe is me" (or a more commonly used statement today "It is me") is accepted as correct in conversation and writing.

Subjective Case Pronouns Used for Subjective Complements

Subjective case pronouns, with an exception discussed in the sidebar, are also used for subjective complements (specifically predicate nominatives). As shown below, with the finite list of subjective pronouns memorized, you can use your diagramming skills to easily determine the proper pronoun.

Note: One way to check your answer is to mentally invert the sentence so that the subjective complement is the subject.

The talented singer is [she, her].

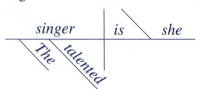

The students who understand the subject are [they, them].

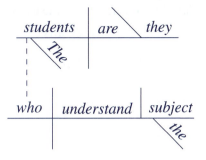

The poets are [she, her] and [he, him].

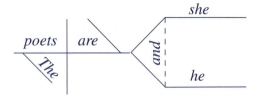

PRACTICE 5-2

Diagram the following sentences to determine the correct personal pronoun. See the appendix for the answers.

1. It is [she, her].

2. It is [she, her] and [he, him].

3. The president is [she, her].

4. The winners are [they, them].

5. The participants in the ceremony are [we, us] and [them, they].

Objective Case Pronouns

Personal pronouns that are used as objects of sentences must use objective case pronouns. The following pronouns can be easily memorized because they include a finite number:

- me

- him

- her

- us

- them

- you

- it

We also know that objects in sentences can be direct objects, indirect objects, and objects of prepositions. With this knowledge and the list on page 73 memorized, we can use diagramming to quickly determine the correct pronoun.

The answer surprised [they, them].

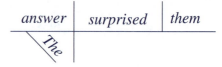

[He, him] gave [she, her] the book.

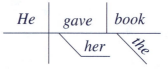

The run exhausted Nancy and [I, me].

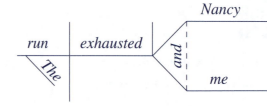

The cowboy shared the campfire with [she, her] and [he, him].

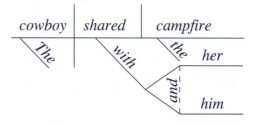

With your diagramming skills and the lists of subjective and objective personal pronouns memorized, you can solve more challenging pronoun use problems as shown in the following example:

Trish competed better than [I, me].

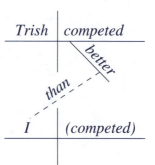

As shown in the diagram, the pronoun is the subject of the adverb clause. This pronoun has an implied (not stated) verb—*competed*. Therefore, the pronoun must be in the subjective case. One way to double-check your choice is to verbally complete the sentence: Trish competed better than I competed.

PRACTICE 5-3

Diagram the following sentences to determine the correct pronoun use. The answers are in the appendix.

1. Wanda shared the news with [they, them].

2. The news was given to [me, I] and [him, he].

3. They showed [him, he] and [she, her] the x-ray.

4. The book was read by [us, we] readers.

5. The doctors gave [him, he] the news about [they, them].

Possessive Case Pronouns

As the name implies, **possessive case** pronouns show ownership or relationship. Again, the forms are finite in number. The following possessive pronouns function as adjectives (and are placed before nouns):

■ Their—*Their* talent is obvious.

■ My—*My* respect is sincere.

■ Your—*Your* review is accurate.

■ Our—*Our* people will call your people.

■ Her—*Her* review gave the author chills.

■ His—This is *his* second Broadway play.

■ Its—The play won an award for *its* costumes.

The following possessive pronouns function as subjects, direct objects, and subjective complements:

■ Theirs—*Theirs* is a simple life.

■ Mine—The choice is *mine*.

■ Yours—The decision is *yours*.

■ Ours—*Ours* is the brown cat.

- Hers—*Hers* was the best design in the contest.

- His—*His* was the best paper in the contest.

- Its—*Its* is a possessive pronoun.

Notice how *his* and *its* function as both pronouns and adjectives.

Rule

Its is a possessive pronoun.

> The journal shared *its* secrets.

> *It's* with an apostrophe is a contraction meaning *it is.*

To distinguish the two types, say "it is." If this makes sense in the sentence, you have a contraction. If it does not make sense, you have a possessive pronoun; do not use the apostrophe for a possessive pronoun.

Proper use of possessive pronouns is easy to identify from our natural speech with one exception. If a pronoun modifies a gerund, it needs the possessive form as shown below. (See Chapter 6 for an explanation of a gerund.)

[You, your] winning the race means everything to them.

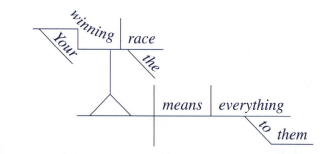

PRACTICE 5-4

Diagram the following sentences to determine the correct pronoun use.

1. [Their, theirs] tree house is theirs.

2. [You, your] solution to the problem is brilliant.

3. The nurse remembered [you, your] chart.

4. The brick house on the corner is [my, mine].

5. The brick house on the corner is [my, mine] house.

Reflexive and Intensive Pronouns

A **reflexive pronoun** is a type of personal pronoun that refers back to an antecedent in the same sentence—often the subject of the sentence. A reflexive pronoun cannot be the subject of a sentence. It can refer back only to the subject, and the noun or pronoun it refers back to needs to be in the same sentence to ensure clarity.

Scott gave *himself* the injection.

Notice the entirely different meaning below if an objective case pronoun is substituted for the reflexive pronoun:

Scott gave *him* the injection.

In the first sentence above, Scott is giving himself the shot. In the second sentence, he is giving someone else the shot. This example shows how important reflexive pronouns are for sentence clarity.

The reflexive pronouns are identified below:

Viewpoint	Singular	Plural
First Person	myself	ourselves
Second Person	yourself	yourselves
Third Person	himself, herself, itself	themselves

Notice how all of the reflexive pronouns end with either -self or -selves.

In addition to referring back to the subject, reflective pronouns can be used for emphasis. When used for emphasis, these reflexive pronouns are called **intensive pronouns.**

I can eat that banana split *myself.*

They finished the race *themselves.*

Let's answer all the questions *ourselves.*

Note: It is easy to identify intensive pronouns because the pronoun can be removed from the sentence with the sentence still remaining clear.

A key to using reflexive and intensive pronouns correctly is to understand that they are never used as the subject of a sentence. For example, the following is incorrect:

Howard and myself traveled through the desert.

The correct sentence reads as follows:

Howard and I traveled through the desert.

Another key to using reflexive pronouns correctly is to understand that they need to have the proper antecedent in the same sentence. The following examples are incorrect:

Negotiations are continuing between *ourselves* and the union.
(Ask yourself if *ourselves* refers back to negotiations.)

The company is impressed with workers like *yourself*.
(Again, ask if *yourself* refers back to company.)

The correct sentences read as follows:

Negotiations are continuing between *us* and the union.

The company is impressed with workers like *you*.

In the incorrect sentences, the reflexive pronoun has no noun to refer back to.

PRACTICE 5-5

Diagram the following sentences to determine the correct pronoun use. The answers are in the appendix.

1. Lisa and [I, me, myself] biked through the hills.

2. John needs the medicine. John gave [him, himself] a shot.

3. The employees received the paperwork and allowed [them, they, themselves] time for comprehension.

4. The rules are clear between [us, ourselves] and the other team.

5. Your brother looks like [you, yourself].

Indefinite Pronouns

A way to remember the definition of **indefinite pronouns** is to know that these are pronouns that do not refer to a definite person or thing, hence the term indefinite. Also, these pronouns are unique in that they usually do not have antecedents.

Like other types of pronouns, the list of indefinite pronouns is finite, and the most common ones are shown below.

Singular Indefinite Pronouns				Plural	Singular or Plural
another	anybody	anyone	anything	both	all
each	either	everybody	everyone	few	any
everything	little	much	neither	many	more
nobody	no one	nothing	one	others	most
other	somebody	someone	something	several	none
					some

The indefinite pronouns listed above as singular *must* take a singular verb. Those listed above as plural *must* take a plural verb. Those listed as either singular or plural take a singular or plural verb depending on the context of the sentence.

> Anyone *is* invited.
>
> *Both* plan to attend.
>
> All of the guests *are* arriving.
>
> All of the paper *is* blue.

Know that sometimes the words in the table above are used as adjective-noun combinations. In these cases, the two-word combinations are spelled not as one word but as two words, as in the example: *Every one* of you is bright. Most often with the two-word combinations, you will be using the indefinite pronoun instead of an adjective-noun combination. One way to recognize the adjective-noun combination is that the preposition *of* often follows the combination.

In addition to subject and verb agreement, an important thing to learn about indefinite pronouns is how to use them properly (based on if they are singular or plural) with other pronouns.

> Everyone gives [his, their] best.

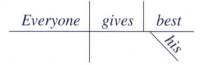

The problem with this sentence is that everyone is singular and the pronoun being used as an adjective—his—must agree in number with its antecedent (everyone). *Their* is not correct because it is plural and *everyone* is a singular pronoun. Obviously, solving the grammar problem causes a new problem. In many circumstances, *everyone* will include males and females, so the *his* reference is grammatically correct but gender incorrect. One way to solve this problem is to write: Everyone gives his or her best.

PRACTICE 5-6

Diagram the following sentences with indefinite pronouns to determine the correct verb use.

1. Everything in the store [is, are] on sale.

2. Everyone in the buildings [knows, know] the evacuation route.

3. Each of the paintings [is, are] valuable.

4. Many on the team [plan, plans] for their college education.

5. Most of the players [is, are] juniors.

Demonstrative Pronouns

Demonstrative pronouns are used to point to a noun. Here are the singular and plural forms.

Singular Form	Plural Form
This	These
That	Those

These pronouns often function as adjectives (*that* apple) or substitutes for nouns. (*This* is the day.)

Use *this* and *these* when referring to things that are nearby in area or time.

> *This* is my dog on the porch.
>
> *These* are beautiful flowers that you are selling.
>
> *This* dog on your porch is well trained.
>
> *These* flowers that you are selling are beautiful.

Use *that* and *those* when referring to things that are farther away in area or time.

> *That* is his dog on the porch across the street.
>
> *Those* are beautiful flowers at the other store.

That dog on your neighbor's porch is well trained.

Those flowers at the other store are beautiful.

Relative Pronouns

To understand how to diagram relative pronouns and to know more about their functions within sentences, please read about adjective clauses in Chapter 4.

Relative pronouns introduce dependent clauses that function as adjectives. The relative pronouns are as follows:

that, which, and *who* (including *whom* and *whose* as forms of *who*)

These pronouns "relate"—or refer back—to the noun at their immediate left, which is called the antecedent (as shown in the examples below).

For the relative pronoun *who* in the sentence—The dog owner, *who* walks that dog with floppy ears, is my brother—the antecedent is *owner* (i.e., the word *who* refers back to).

For the relative pronoun *whom* in the sentence—The dog fetches tennis balls from his owner **whom** *the dog adores*—the antecedent is *owner*.

For the relative pronoun *which* in the sentence—The tennis balls, **which** *sometimes fly over my fence*, are chewed and soiled—the antecedent is *balls*.

For the relative pronoun *that* in the sentence—They are used tennis balls **that** *the dog chases*—the antecedent is *balls*.

Note in all the examples above that the antecedent is the word that immediately precedes the relative pronoun.

Rule

How to decide what relative pronoun—*that, which, who, whom*, or *whose*—to use with specific antecedents.

Who, whom, and **whose** are used when referring back to people. (Stated in a more technical way: **Who, whom**, and **whose** have antecedents that are people.) See below for an explanation of when to use who and whom.

That and **which** are used when referring back to objects, animals, or ideas. (**That** and **which** have antecedents that are objects, animals, or ideas.)

Where is used to refer back to nouns of location. (**Where** has antecedents that are locations.)

As you have just learned, relative pronouns function within the adjective clause as either a subject, adjective, direct object, or object of a preposition. Here are some examples that can be seen clearly in the diagrams. (To understand how to diagram these adjective clauses, please review Chapter 4.)

Relative pronoun as a subject:

The car *that is speeding down the street* is red.

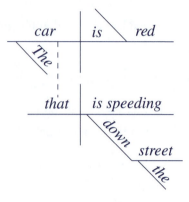

In the dependent clause *that is speeding down the street*, "that" functions as a subject.

Relative pronoun as an adjective:

My youngest son, *whose friend owns a car*, is driving with him to school.

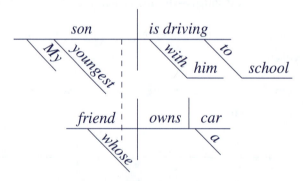

In the dependent clause *whose friend owns a car*, "whose" is acting as an adjective.

Relative pronoun as a direct object:

The coat *that you forgot* is in the hall closet.

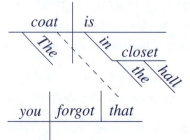

In the dependent clause *that you forgot*, "that" is acting as the direct object of "you forgot."

Relative pronoun as the object of a preposition:

The teacher of *whom you spoke* is my mentor.

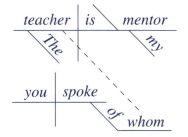

The dependent clause *whom you spoke* is the object of the preposition "of."

Relative pronouns omitted:

Sometimes in a sentence the relative pronoun is omitted because it is understood, but this understood pronoun still serves its usual functions. For example

The tickets I needed were sold out.

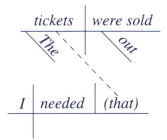

The tickets [that] I needed were sold out.

Rule

Understanding When to Use Who or Whom

It is only in relative pronouns that *who* changes form. (As stated previously, the relative pronouns *who, whose, whom, which,* and *that* attach adjective clauses to their antecedent—the noun or pronoun modified.)

Who, a subjective case pronoun, can be used only for subjects and subjective complements.

Whom, an objective case pronoun, can be used only for objects.

1. Here are the rules: Use *who* or *whoever* when the pronoun is the subject of the verb.

    Whoever is knocking at the door?

    I question *who* wrote these directions.

    I trust *whoever* signed the check.

2. Use *who* or *whoever* when the pronoun is the subjective complement.

> The masked rider was *who?*

> No one knew *who* the masked rider was.

> The winner was *whoever* finished first.

3. Use *whom* or *whomever* when the pronoun is the direct object of a verb or the object of a preposition.

> *Whom* did he select?

> He can select *whomever* he wants.

> With *whom* were you talking?

4. At the beginning of *who/whom* questions, use *who* if the question is about the subject, or *whom* if the question is about the object.

Practice with *Who* and *Whom*

1. From (who, whom) did you get those flowers?

2. (Who, Whom) is your friend?

3. The company selected (who, whom) for the honor?

4. (Who, Whom) knows how to use this new VCR?

5. No one knew (who, whom) gave us the flowers.

6. A tough one: Give this work to (whoever, whomever) looks bored.

Answers:

1. Whom (object of the preposition "from")

2. Who (subject of the verb)

3. Whom (direct object of the verb)

4. Who (subject of the verb)

5. Who (subjective complement)

6. Whoever (subject of "looks bored"; the object of the preposition "to" is the entire clause "whoever looks bored.")

Interrogative Pronouns

The **interrogative pronouns**—*what, which,* and *who* (including the forms *whom* and *whose)*—ask questions. These pronouns have no antecedent.

>*What* time is it?

>*Which* time zone are we in?

>*Who* knows the time?

>*Whom* are we asking?

>*Whose* watch is that?

Use *who, whom,* and *whose* for asking questions about people.

>*Who* wrote that beautiful poem?

>*Whose* poem is that?

>*Whom* are we discussing?

Notice, as we learned earlier, that *who* is used for the nominative case (for the subject), and *whom* is used for the objective case.

Use *which* for identifying a few or one out of a larger group.

>*Which* piece of candy do you want?

>*Which* man is he?

>*Which* kitten is the smallest?

Use *what* to ask for a description.

>*What* is the answer?

>*What* photos do you want?

>*What* did the explorers discover?

Reciprocal Pronouns

Many grammar books do not even mention these pronoun phrases—*each other* and *one another.*

Use *each other* when referring to a group of only two people, animals, or things.

>The two grandmothers shared stories about *each other's* grandchildren.

>The male and female chimpanzees helped *each other* climb over the wall.

Use *one another* when referring to a group of more than two.

The bicycle racers will help *one another* win the race.

The five chimpanzees climbed over *one another* while playing.

COMPREHENSIVE PRACTICE 5–7

Practice diagramming these sentences containing examples from each of the lessons in Chapter 5. You will also need to select the correct pronoun or verb for each sentence. Check your answers in the appendix.

1. She and [he, him] watched the sunset.

2. Peter and [her, she] celebrated the victory.

3. Her relatives, Sam and [he, him], are in the photo.

4. Everybody in the databases [is, are] on the master list.

5. [She, her] and [them, they] watched the movie.

6. The winner is [she, her].

7. The painting on the wall is [my, mine].

8. My friend is [he, him].

9. The painting on the wall is [my, mine] painting.

10. The scientists who discovered the protein are [they, them].

11. Linda's favorite librarians provided [she, her] and [he, him] the files.

12. Spot and [I, myself] hiked in the valley.

13. It is [they, them].

14. Negotiations occurred between [us, ourselves] and the union.

15. Those responsible are [we, us] and [them, they].

16. Gene needs insulin. Gene gave [him, himself] a shot.

17. [She, her] gave [he, him] the directions.

18. The committee questioned [he, him] and [I, me].

19. Everything in the bags [is, are] for the garage sale.

20. Each of the flowers [is, are] rare.

Chapter 6

Verbals

Verbals are words formed from verbs but used as other parts of speech. The three types of verbals are participles, gerunds, and infinitives.

- The **participle** is a word formed from a verb and used like an adjective.

- The **gerund** is a word formed from a verb and used like a noun.

- The **infinitive** is a word formed from a verb and used like a noun, an adjective, or an adverb.

> ### Learning Objectives for Chapter 6
>
> After studying this chapter, you will be able to
>
> - Define, recognize, and diagram the three types of verbals: participles, gerunds, and infinitives
> - Recognize and solve dangling participle errors

Note: In reference to verbals, which are words formed from verbs but used as other parts of speech, the *participle* is a verb form used like an adjective. However, in reference to the form and tense of a verb, the participle (both present and past) is used with a helping verb to indicate tense, aspect, or voice, as we will review in the next chapter on verbs.

The Participle

In reference to verbals, the participle is a verb form used like an adjective. It modifies a noun or a pronoun. Present participles end in –ing. Past participles often end in –d, -ed, -t, or –en.

Present Participles	Past Participles
growling dog	*realized* value
singing telegram man	*abandoned* idea
living history	*destroyed* property

In the example above, growling is an adjective because it tells something about the dog, but it is formed from the verb *growl*. Therefore, it is a participle. It is formed from a verb and is used like an adjective.

Notice in the examples just given that the participle is simply one word. In the example below, the participle has modifiers; hence, the participle and its modifiers are known as a **participial phrase**.

Having won the race, the student celebrated.

Having won is formed from the verb *won* and modifies *student*; it is therefore a participle. What about the words *the race*? *Having won* what? *The race. Race* is the object of the participle *having won.*

Present Participle Phrases

The student *winning the race* is John.

Carrying the award, the student walked proudly.

They interviewed the hikers *climbing in the canyon.*

Past Participle Phrases

The stone *mined in Africa* is worth millions.

The book *located in the antique shop* is a first edition book.

The statues *situated throughout the campus* are beautiful.

Diagramming Participles and Participle Phrases

Because the participle is a modifying word, it must be connected in the diagram to the word it modifies, as shown in the diagram below.

Carrying the award, the student walked proudly.

Step 1:

Diagram the subject and verb.

Step 2:

Diagram the modifiers, including the participle and its modifiers.

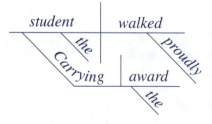

Notice how the participle is placed on a line that looks like the prepositional phrase line. The lines may look the same, but the function and meaning are completely different (like the difference between a prepositional phrase and an indirect object). In addition, the words are placed in different places on the line. Whereas the preposition is placed on the diagonal line, the participle is curved between the diagonal and horizontal line as shown above.

Here are a few more examples:

Jerry answered the question, hoping for extra credit.

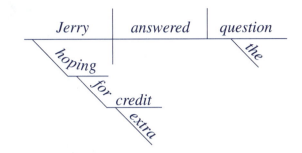

They interviewed the climbers hiking in the canyon.

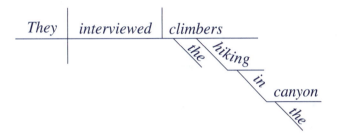

The book located in the antique shop is a first-edition book.

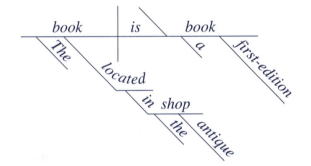

Template for diagramming participles.

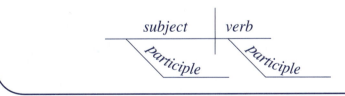

Rule

The **dangling participle problem** causes sentences to be unclear. For example,

Driving through the park, the waterfalls could be seen. (dangling participle problem) Notice how this sentence reads as if the waterfall is doing the driving.

Driving through the park, I saw the waterfalls. (corrected)

When a participle phrase is placed as the beginning of a sentence, it must modify the subject of the sentence that follows, as shown in the corrected example above. In other words, the dangling participle problem is solved by placing the participle next to the subject that it modifies, as shown in another example:

Running the marathon, the spectators cheered Brad as he finished mile 20. (dangling participle problem)

Notice how this sentence reads as if the spectators are running the marathon. (Although a grammatical problem, we are fairly certain Brad wouldn't mind having this problem at mile 20!)

Running a marathon, Brad passed cheering spectators at mile 20. (corrected)

PRACTICE 6-1

Practice your new skill by diagramming the following sentences containing participle phrases. The answers are in the appendix.

1. A seal swimming in the cold sea is comfortable.

2. Focusing on the road, the young driver missed the exit.

3. Thrilled by their work, the teacher praised the students.

4. The horse galloping through Main Street caused a commotion.

5. The signs located throughout the city garden provide the names of flowers.

Gerund

The **gerund** is formed from a verb and used like a noun. Therefore, it can act in a sentence as a subject, direct object, object of a preposition, subjective complement, or appositive. The gerund always ends in *–ing*.

Painting is hard work.

In the sentence above, the verb is *is*. *Painting* is the subject of *is*. *Painting* is formed from a verb and used as a noun; therefore, *painting* is a gerund.

Terry excelled in *painting*.

In is a preposition and *painting* is its object; *painting* therefore is a gerund because it is formed from a verb and used as a noun.

Terry's favorite activity is *painting*.

Painting tells what Terry's favorite activity is; therefore, it explains the subject. It is a subjective complement. Notice that *painting* is not part of the verb; *activity* and *painting* refer to the same thing.

Here are some more sentences containing gerunds and gerund phrases:

> *Sleeping* is essential to good health. (subject)
>
> She loves *sleeping* late into the morning. (direct object)
>
> Her favorite relaxation is *sleeping*. (subjective complement)
>
> The futon is used for *sleeping*. (object of preposition)

Diagramming Gerunds and Gerund Phrases

A gerund is not a modifying word; it is essential to the completeness of a sentence. Therefore, it is diagrammed within the core of the sentence as a subject, direct object, object of a preposition, subjective complement, or appositive, as shown in the examples below:

> Painting a picture is fun.

Step 1:

Draw a stand on the baseline of the sentence where the gerund functions in the sentence. As shown below, place the gerund going down a one-step line, from the top and to the base of the step.

Step 2:

Diagram any modifiers.

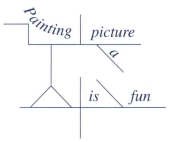

> Terry's favorite activity is painting.

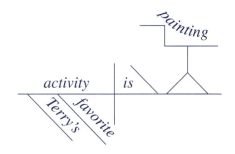

Terry excels in painting landscapes.

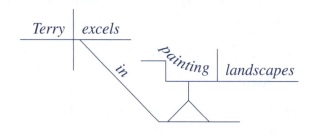

Terry enjoys painting landscapes.

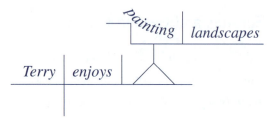

Terry's talent, painting pictures, is recognized nationally.

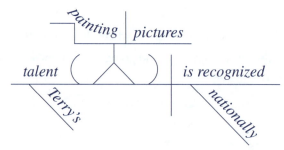

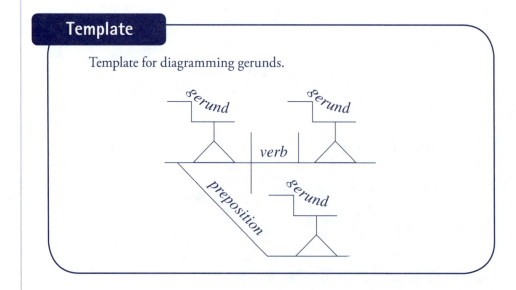

Now try your skill diagramming these practice sentences. The answers are in the appendix.

1. Studying is necessary for a good grade.

2. She enjoys studying in the early morning.

3. Her favorite school activity is studying with friends.

4. This textbook is used for studying grammar.

5. Her favorite activity, studying with friends, is a challenge.

Infinitives

An **infinitive** is a verb form used as an adjective, adverb, or noun (including the functions of nouns such as subjects, direct objects, objects of prepositions, subjective complements, and appositives).

The infinitive is easy to recognize because it is preceded by the word *to*.

Note: Do not confuse an infinitive with a prepositional phrase introduced by *to*. In an infinitive, *to* is followed by a verb form. (*To sleep* is my favorite indulgence.) In the prepositional phrase, *to* is followed by a noun or a pronoun. (She gave the directions *to me*.)

Infinitives Functioning as Nouns

> *To sing* soothes the soul.

To sing is used as the subject of soothes. *Sing* is a verb form; it is preceded by *to*. *To sing* is an infinitive used as the subject of *soothes*.

> She likes *to sing*.

Here *sing* is an infinitive used as the direct object.

> Her passion is *to sing*.

The above infinitive is used as a subjective complement.

Infinitives Functioning as Adjectives and Adverbs

> The flowers *to sell* are in the red bucket.

To sell tells which flowers and is an infinitive used as an adjective.

> We met *to share* the meal.

To share is an infinitive used as an adverb. It tells why we met.

Diagramming Infinitives

Diagramming Infinitive Phrases Functioning as Nouns

Step 1:

Place the infinitive on a stand in the position where it functions in the sentence. At the top of the stand, diagram the infinitive marker (*to*) on a slanted line (just like with a preposition). Diagram the infinitive on the horizontal line connected to the stand. Finish diagramming the rest of the sentence.

To garden is pure joy.

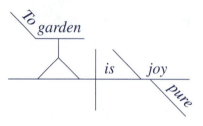

He loves *to garden* in the summer mornings.

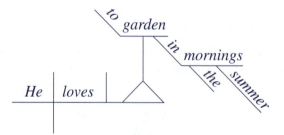

His favorite activity is *to garden*.

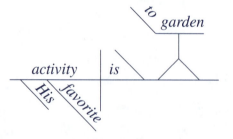

Template

Template for diagramming infinitives functioning as nouns.

Diagramming Infinitives and Infinitive Phrases
Functioning as Adjectives and Adverbs

As you know, adjectives and adverbs are diagrammed under the word on the horizontal baseline that they modify. The infinitive or infinitive phrase used as an adjective or adverb also is diagrammed under the word on the horizontal baseline that it modifies.

The albums *to give* graduates are at the printer.

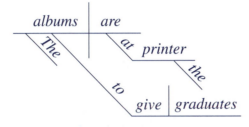

They planned *to help* the team.

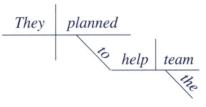

The student government met to decide the fate of the proposed club.

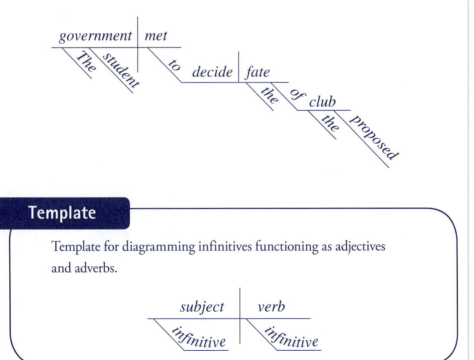

Template

Template for diagramming infinitives functioning as adjectives and adverbs.

PRACTICE 6-3

Now try your skill diagramming infinitives functioning as nouns, adjectives, and adverbs. The answers are in the appendix.

1. To sew well takes real patience.

2. Her passion is to sing country music.

3. The car to buy is on the lot.

4. We met with the team to discuss our plan.

5. The new product to watch is designed to save money.

COMPREHENSIVE PRACTICE 6-4

Practice diagramming these sentences containing examples from each of the lessons in Chapter 6. Check your answers in the appendix.

1. To speak well of others is a true gift.

2. Fishing for big bass is my hobby.

3. Recognizing her grandmother, the child ran into her arms.

4. Waking from little sleep, the student stumbled into the shower.

5. They love to discuss protein synthesis.

6. I love fishing for bass.

7. A hard lesson to learn is that one.

8. The treasure located on the map with an X has remained buried for centuries.

9. He planned to share his success with others.

10. Writing is one way to understand an issue.

11. The truck driver enjoys singing with the radio.

12. The cookies to bring them are in the freezer.

13. Amazed by their talent, the art dealer sponsored their show.

14. The detective followed the car speeding through the streets.

15. We collected bottles to earn money for the trip.

16. Learning to drive a clutch is easy in retrospect.

17. Practicing the guitar takes time.

18. His profession, singing opera, requires dedication.

19. Running to catch the bus, Pam forgot her project to share with the class.

20. Wishing on the first night star, he hoped to gain any advantage.

Chapter 7

Verbs

In previous chapters, we have relied on diagramming to teach the basic functions of the parts of speech. This technique is effective for teaching these functions because diagramming shows visually how words function and relate within a sentence. For example, we know now that the word *paint* can function as a subject or a verb in a sentence depending on how it is used. (The *paint* is dry. Let's *paint* the fence.)

With some exceptions, which are illustrated with diagrams in this chapter, the more complex points of verbs simply need to be memorized. Therefore, this chapter is more like a reference chapter and less like the previous diagramming chapters.

Some of this information repeats information in previous chapters (like the difference between linking and action verbs) because you needed to know that information within the specific chapter, but it is also provided here for easier reference.

> ## Learning Objectives for Chapter 7
>
> After studying this chapter, you will be able to
>
> - Define and recognize action, linking, and helping verbs
> - Understand the proper use of specific transitive and intransitive verbs, such as rise, raise, sit, set, lie, and lay
> - Understand the number and person of verbs
> - Diagram inverted sentences (those beginning with *there*)
> - Define, recognize, and diagram active and passive sentences
> - Define, recognize, and diagram subjective mood sentences
> - Understand and properly use the forms and tenses of verbs

We placed this overview about verbs as the last chapter in this book because verbs, although absolutely essential, could overwhelm the beginning grammar student. One way to use this chapter is in parallel with the other chapters. In this way, you can move along through the other chapters and pull from this verb chapter information as it becomes important in your journey.

The Verb Defined

A **verb** shows action, links another word to the subject, helps another verb, or shows existence.

She *ran.*	(*Ran* shows action.)
She *is* a good runner.	(*Is* links the subject to the subjective complement *runner.*)
She is *running* a good race.	(*Is* helps the other verb *running.*)
She is alive.	(*Is* shows existence.)

Another word for verb is simple predicate. The complete predicate is the verb and all the other words that describe or limit it.

Types of Verbs—Action, Linking, and Helping

Action Verbs

An **action verb** usually describes physical or mental action.

> The student *read* the book.
>
> I *rise* with the morning sun.
>
> The fire alarm *awoke* the neighbors.
>
> Brenda *delivered* the morning papers.
>
> Nathan *lay* the papers on the counter.
>
> I *lie* on the beach.
>
> I *believe* the news.
>
> We *realize* his sincerity.

Action verbs are further divided into **transitive** and **intransitive verbs**.

- **Transitive verbs**—those verbs followed by a direct object. A way to remember this is that transitive verbs "transfer" their action down to another word—the direct object.

- **Intransitive verbs**—those verbs that are not followed by a direct object.

A direct object follows the verb in the sentence and answers "what" about the verb; it receives the action of the verb or shows the recipient of the action of the verb. For details about how to identify and diagram direct objects, see Chapter 2.

Understanding the difference between an intransitive and transitive verb is important in avoiding some of the commonly confused verbs. For example, the intransitive verb *rise* means "to get up" and the transitive verb *raise* means "to lift." Both are close in spelling but far away in meaning. Some of these commonly confused verbs are diagrammed here after their definition.

Definition: *To rise* is an intransitive verb that means to get up or ascent.

> I rise in the morning.

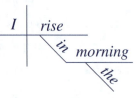

Definition: *To raise* is a transitive verb meaning to lift or cause to rise.

I raise corn in the garden.

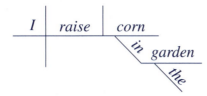

Definition: *To sit* is an intransitive verb that means to be seated.

I sit in the blue chair.

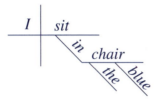

Definition: *To set* is a transitive verb that means to put or place.

I set the red roses on the blue chair.

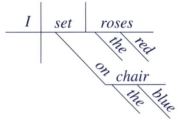

Definition: *To lie* is an intransitive verb meaning to recline.

You lie on the beach.

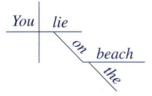

Definition: *To lay* is a transitive verb meaning to put or place.

You lay the towel on the sand.

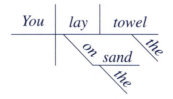

Linking Verbs

Linking verbs are a type of verb that connects or links the subject to its complement. Linking verbs describe the subject—meaning the same thing as the subject; they do not perform any action. See Chapter 2 for more information about subjective complements and the role of linking verbs in their function.

As listed in the following table, the verb form *to be* is the most common example of a linking verb. Memorizing these linking verbs is recommended.

Linking verbs from the verb form *to be*	
am	were
is	be
are	being
was	been

The clouds *are* dark and gray.

I *am* relaxed.

She *is* nice.

The flowers *are* beautiful.

That *was* a long trip.

Rule

"To be or not to be"—The "Be" verb—a Quick Clarification

If you haven't studied a foreign language, you may not understand what someone means when they say "the *to be* or *be* verb." This verb is the base form of the following eight forms:

Be, am, is, are, was, were, being, been

The *be* verb can be used as a linking verb or a helping verb. A linking verb connects the verb to a subjective complement. A helping verb occurs before a main verb and helps that verb express action. (She was *giving* a speech to the class.)

As you know, it is difficult to get through a day without using a *to be* verb.

Other linking verbs express sense perception such as sight, smell, taste, sound, and feel.

The vet *looked* professional.

The dog *smelled* skunky.

The strawberries *tasted* fresh.

The child's cry *sounded* sad.

I *feel* good.

These sense perception verbs are limited in number (which makes them easy to memorize), as shown in the following table:

Linking verbs other than the *to be* form	
taste	feel
smell	sound
look	grow
sound	appear
become	seem
remain	stay

Note that the same word can be a linking verb and an action verb, but the word has different meanings.

Linking verb: The chime *sounded* loud. (Loud is an adjective, and functions as a subjective complement, which refers back to the subject—linking the subject to the complement.)

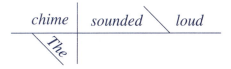

Action verb: The chime *sounded* the opening act.

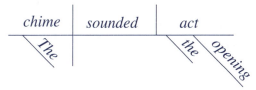

The linking verb "*sounded*" describes the chime—how it sounded. The chime in this case is not performing the action. The action verb "*sounded*" describes something the chime does.

Helping (or Auxiliary) Verbs

As we just reviewed, linking verbs link subjects to subjective complements. These linking verbs are limited in number and are most often in a form of the verb *to be*: is, am, are, was, were, being, been.

Helping verbs help the main verb by showing time, providing emphasis, or noting possibility. Helping verbs (or **auxiliary verbs**) also include the forms of the verb *to be*; however, the purpose of the helping verb is different from a linking verb. As the name implies, the helping verb helps a main verb; therefore, it is always the first verb of a verb combination (a verb phrase).

Time—They *are* waiting for a table.
Time—They *were* waiting for a table.

Emphasis—The baseball player *does* sign all the autographs.
Emphasis—The vacuum *will* clean muddy footprints.

Possibility—Pat *could* win the race.
Possibility—Terry m*ight* finish the marathon.

The following table lists the limited number of helping verbs:

Helping verbs		
To be verbs	Forms of *have* and *do*	Modal verbs—refer to an action in the future
am	have	shall
is	has	will
are	had	should
was	do	would
were	does	may
be	did	might
being		must
been		can
		could

It is important to remember when diagramming helping verbs to diagram all the verbs in the phrase in the verb position of the diagram, as in the following examples:

She is *excelling* in math.

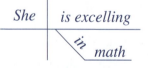

No team *can win* forever.

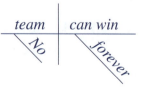

©2008 by Marye Hefty, Sallie Ortiz, Sara Nelson

The team *did finish* the race.

One of the challenges of diagramming a helping verb is that adverbs often interrupt the verb phrase. You diagram these adverbs at their correct place in the diagram as shown in the following examples:

The team *did* not *finish* the game.

No team *can* always *win* each race.

Modal Verbs

Helping verbs that refer to some action in the future are called **modal verbs**.

There are five modal verbs with the following forms:

Base and present form	Past form
can	could
may	might
must	(no form)
shall	should
will	should

I *can go* to the game tomorrow.
I *could go* with you next week.

He *may run* for president.
He *might run* for president.

The seniors *must pass* the class to graduate.

We *shall prepare* for the meeting.
We *should prepare* for the meeting.

I *will drive.*
I *would drive* if I had my license.

Note: Simple tense changes in modal verbs result in completely different meanings, as illustrated by these two sentences:

> We *shall prepare* for the meeting. (States a certainty)
>
> We *should prepare* for the meeting. (States it is known as needed)

Can, may, shall, and *will* all imply more of a certainty that the event will happen than *could, might, should,* or *would,* which have a more conditional meaning.

Number/Person

Verbs must agree in number. This simply means a singular subject has a singular verb (e.g., he sings—not incorrectly he sing) and a plural subject has a plural verb (e.g., they sing—not they sings).

Person is who or what is receiving (experiencing) the action. Below you can see that the form of the verb changes depending on who or what is the subject.

Notice that when the subject is singular—he, she, or it—the verb has an *s* at its end.

Singular, first person =	I	I see.		
Singular, second person =	you	You see.		
Singular, third person =	he, she, it	He sees.	She sees.	It sees.

Notice that when the subject is plural—we, you, they—the verb has no s at its end. As native English speakers, we intuitively understand this concept.

Plural, first person =	we	We see.
Plural, second person =	you	You see.
Plural, third person =	they	They see.

When the subject of a sentence is a pronoun, the following rules apply:

Pronouns that require that their verbs end in –s	Pronouns that require no s in their verbs
He (drives)	I (drive)
She (drives)	You (drive)
It (drives)	We (drive)

PRACTICE 7-1

In the following sentences, select the correct verb. The answers are in the appendix.

1. He [enjoy, enjoys] music.

2. They [love, loves] to fish.

3. Jacob [read, reads] science fiction into the night.

4. Lisa and John [study, studies] into the night.

5. Anna [diagram, diagrams] in her sleep.

6. The grammar group [learn, learns] for fun.

7. The students and the teacher [learn, learns] for fun.

8. It [float, floats] with a floatation device.

9. You [select, selects] the music.

10. We [take, takes] music lessons.

Not all verb agreement is determined by adding or deleting *s*. The irregular verb *to be* uses *is* as a singular verb in the present tense—He is my friend. She is my friend too. *Are* is used for plural verbs in the present tense—They are friends.

Number/Person Related to Inverted Sentences

Sentences beginning with *there* are called **inverted sentences** because *there* is not the subject; instead, the noun after the verb is the subject. Although *there* is classified as an adverb in such a sentence, it is not considered essential to the sentence. Therefore, it is diagrammed on its own line above the sentence as shown below:

There are a million reasons.

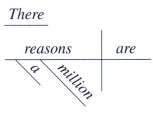

So, in sentences beginning with *there,* make sure the verb agrees in number with the subject that follows it.

There are cows jumping over the moon.

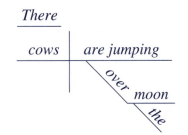

There is a cow jumping over the moon.

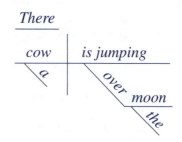

Active and Passive Voice

"Avoid passive voice" is a familiar command to writing students, and this is usually good advice. **Active voice** is preferred because it requires stronger verbs and is more concise. However, sometimes passive voice is perfectly acceptable and even required, as it is in some scientific journals. Therefore, here is the information you'll need to make a basic voice decision, and we'll leave the voice decision up to you. (Do note that when you hear a teacher or peer talk about writing sentences in "the subject/verb/modifier" form, this is another way of recognizing the "active voice" form.)

The two voice choices are active and passive. In an active voice sentence, the subject performs the action of the verb.

1. A dog bit Jim.

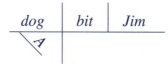

2. Mary gave Pat a birthday gift.

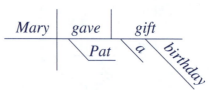

3. I love to write.

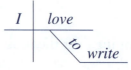

In a **passive voice** sentence, the subject receives the action.

1. Jim was bitten by a dog.

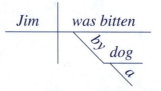

2. Pat was given a birthday gift by Mary.

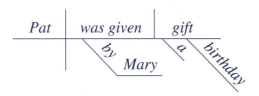

3. Writing is loved by me.

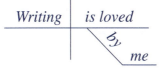

Here are some other examples of active and passive sentences.

Active: The law student aced the exam.
Passive: The exam was aced by the law student. (The subject of the sentence—exam—is not doing the action of acing the exam.)

Active: My dog bit the mailman.
Passive: The mailman was bitten by my dog.

Active: The students demanded higher wages.
Passive: Higher wages were demanded by the students.

Active: Dr. Hyde mixed the red and green solution.
Passive: The red and green solution were mixed.

Try diagramming a few of the above sentences—both active and passive versions. What do you notice?

Yes, the passive sentences are longer and place less emphasis on who performed the action, which is why English teachers tell you to avoid these sentences. However, keep in mind that some scientific journals use passive voice to emphasize the scientific results or process of an experiment and to de-emphasize who performed the experiment.

How to Recognize the Passive Voice

What else do you notice about the passive voice? Well, what you may have noticed in diagramming the above sentences provides tips for recognizing the passive voice. Passive voice sentences always

1. contain a form of the *to be* verb—is, are, was, were, or is being, has been and a past participle, like stung, given, loved, bitten.

A Simple Technique for Recognizing the Passive Voice

If you can place or say the words "by someone" after the verb, then the sentence is in passive voice.

> *The boat was rowed [by someone].*

> *The book was written [by someone].*

I wrote [by someone]. This sentence makes no sense with the added words; therefore, it is active.

Active form	Passive form	
Verb	To Be Verb	+ Past Participle Form
Eat	are, is, was, were, is being, has been	+ eaten
Write	are, is, was, were, is being, has been	+ written
Borrow	are, is, was, were, is being, has been	+ borrowed
Sing	are, is, was, were, is being, has been	+ sung

2. name the doer of the action in a prepositional phrase starting with the preposition *by*. However, sometimes the subject of the sentence is not indicated, as in the sentence: A report was written.

> The boat was rowed **by** me.

> The book was written **by** Harper Lee.

Mood

The **moods** of a verb—indicative, imperative, and subjunctive—show the writer's intent. A verb's mood shows if the writer is expressing a wish, stating a fact, or making a command.

Indicative—Verbs in this mood express statements of fact or opinion or ask a question.

> We all saw the movie.

> What movie did you see?

> We saw *The Wizard of Oz.*

Imperative—Verbs in this mood express statements of command, request, or advise.

> *Watch* the movie!

> *Buy* a large popcorn.

> *See* the matinee.

Verbs in the imperative mood contain an understood subject you, which is the reader/listener of the command or request. This understood subject means that the subject is not included with the sentence (but simply understood as you). You diagram the understood subject *you* in an imperative sentence as follows:

> *Sit* in your seat.

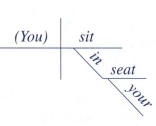

Subjunctive—The subjunctive mood is why it is important to understand moods. Verbs in this mood state a wish, doubt, recommendation, or a condition contrary to fact. Notice what seems to be an obvious subject/verb agreement problem with some of the sentence.

1. It is important that he *be* (not *is*) at the game.

2. The law requires that a certified inspector *replace* (not *replaces*) the contractor.

3. If I *were* a dancer, I would dance until dawn. (not *was*)

Why the Subjunctive Mood Is Important to Understand

The moods of a verb—indicative, imperative, and subjunctive—show the writer's intent. A verb's mood shows if the writer is expressing a wish, stating a fact, or making a command.

Verbs in the subjunctive mood state a wish, doubt, recommendation, or a condition contrary to fact. There are two important facts about the subjunctive mood.

1. Present-tense verbs do not change form to indicate the number and person of the subject. The subjunctive applies the base form of the verb with all subjects (e.g., be, play, sing, and climb).

2. Only one past-tense form of *be* is applied: *were* (never *was*).

Clues for Recognizing the Subjunctive

The subjunctive is found in three situations:

1. In clauses beginning with *if* that are improbable, doubtful, or contrary to fact.

2. In clauses expressing a wish that are improbable, doubtful, or contrary to fact.

3. In noun clauses beginning with the word *that* which make a request, demand, or urging, or showing a necessity or resolution. (The subjunctive is used because the request, demand, or urging has not yet become a reality.)

Some good news: It is easy to identify subjunctive clauses like the ones listed below that begin with *ifs* and *wishes*. You simply look for the clue words: *if* and *wish*.

If I *were* the president, I would declare tomorrow a no-school day.

I wish I *were* going to the prom.

Now here's the even better news: Because you know how to identify and diagram a noun clause, you can easily identify a noun clause beginning with the word *that* which makes a request, demand, or urging that is not yet reality.

"If I were a carpenter..."

*Why is the verb **were** and not **was**?*

In the subjunctive mood, present tense verbs do not show the number and person of the subject. They remain in the base form.

*In the subjunctive mood, past tense verbs use the simple past form. However, for the verb **be**, the word **were** is used for all numbers and persons.*

The students have asked that tomorrow *be* a no-school day (not *is*).

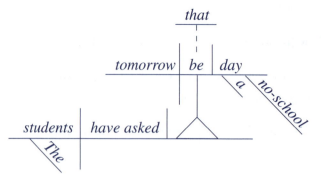

I demand that he *be* selected (not *is*).

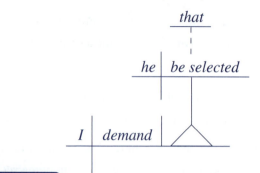

PRACTICE 7-2

In these practice sentences, do the following:

- Identify the mood as indicative (expressing a fact or opinion or asking a question), imperative (expressing a command, request, or advise, and beginning with an implied you subject), or subjunctive.
- Select the correct verb.

1. (You) [watch/watches] the child!

2. The movie [was/were] excellent.

3. If I [was/were] a carpenter and you [was/were] a lady, we would be a famous line in a song.

4. Professor Smith demands that his students [be/are] respectful of others.

5. The demand [be/is] written in a document.

6. (You) [turn/turns] the handle.

7. The formal requests [be/are] in the living will.

8. It is essential that the singers [be/are] ready for the show.

9. I wish she [was/were] the leader.

10. We demanded that he [be taken/is taken] to the specialist.

Forms and Tenses of Verbs

To understand verb tenses (usually thought of as a verb's indication of time), it is important to know the forms of English verbs. Textbooks differ in how many verb forms they define: four, five, or six. Each textbook is correct because it depends on how you slice the verb (e.g., place infinitive and base forms together or apart). The table below lists six forms of regular and irregular verbs.

It is important not to confuse forms with tenses. Verb forms are used to make verb tenses, but forms and tenses are not the same.

	Infinitive	Base	Present simple (third person singular)	Present participle	Past (simple)	Past participle
	begins with *to*	dictionary form	usually ends in *-s*	follows *be* and ends in *-ing*		follows *have*
Regular verbs	to move to love to jump	move love jump	moves loves jumps	moving loving jumping	moved loved jumped	(have) moved (have) loved (have) jumped
Irregular verbs	to build to draw to break	build draw break	builds draws breaks	building drawing breaking	built drew broke	(have) built (have) drawn (have) broken
	to be	be	is, am, are	being	was were	(have) been

Verbs may be classified as regular or irregular depending on how the past and past participle are formed. The irregular verbs differ from the regular verbs only in the past and past participle. (Note that there are thousands of English regular verbs but only about 300 irregular ones.)

Regular verbs form the past and past participle by adding -ed, -d, or -t to the present.

> Loved, moved, jumped, dreamt

Irregular verbs form the past and past participle in irregular ways. (A verb that does not form the past and past participle by adding -ed, -d, or -t to the present is an **irregular verb**.)

Usually, native English speakers intuitively speak and write the irregular forms correctly. However, other than an intuitive sense (from immersion in a language), the irregular verb forms must be memorized to be understood because there is no standard rule to their irregularity.

Here is a partial list of the irregular forms. It is best to memorize these.

Irregular Forms of Verbs

Present	Past	Past Participle
begin	began	(have) begun
broadcast	broadcast (not broadcasted)	(have) broadcast
burst	burst (not bursted)	(have) burst
come	came	(have) come
dive	dove or dived	(have) dove or dived
do	did	(have) done
drink	drank	(have) drunk
drive	drove	(have) driven
eat	ate	(have) eaten
fly	flew	(have) flown
get	got	(have) got
go	went	(have) gone
hang (execute)	hanged	(have) hanged
hang (suspend)	hung	(have) hung
lay (place)	laid	(have) lain
lie (recline)	lay	(have) lain
lie (tell an untruth)	lied	(have) lied
raise (elevate)	raised	(have) raised
rise (become higher)	rose	(have) risen
set (place)	set	(have) set
see	saw	(have) seen
sit (be in a sitting position)	sat	(have) sat

Note: Do not confuse the past with the past participle. The latter always uses the helping verb have/has with the main verb.

Tenses of Verbs

Understanding tenses is like asking for directions. Depending on your reference, you may get different directions to the same place. As an example, read three or four other grammar books about tenses, and you will read different descriptions, definitions, and numbers for tenses, but somehow all these books arrive at the same place: it is important to understand tenses. So, here are our directions.

The first challenge with tenses is the definition. Many grammar books define tense as indicating the time of an action in relation to the speaking or writing of that action. The problem with this definition is that, as you will soon see, present tense does not always refer to present time.

So, why do we use such an inexact system? We do because our grammar study historically comes from the study of Latin, and in the Latin language, the tensing of verbs is logical. Unfortunately, we have applied this system and vocabulary to the English language, and all the definitions don't fit. What does this mean? As in your study of calculus, you will simply need to memorize the formulas, and with more advanced study you can hope it all makes sense.

The good news is that understanding the forms of a verb help us remember the correct tenses of a verb.

There are six tenses in English and six progressive modes.

- Present tense
- Past tense
- Future tense (*will* or *shall* + the present)
- Present perfect tense (*have* or *has* + the past participle)
- Past perfect tense (*had* + the past participle)
- Future perfect tense (will have or shall have + the past participle)

Note that the following "modes" are for all practical purposes "tenses." However, for historical reasons (related to the study of English using a Latin structure), the modes are not called tenses, so we'll continue to call them modes.

- Present progressive mode (*is* or *are* + present participle)
- Past progressive mode (*was* or *were* + present participle)
- Future progressive mode (*will be* or *shall be* + present participle)
- Present perfect progressive mode (*has been* or *have been* + present participle)
- Past perfect progressive mode (*had been* + present participle)
- Future perfect progressive mode (*will have been* + present participle)

The following table is a conjugation of the verb *learn*. To conjugate a verb means to determine and list how the various tenses are formed, as shown on the next page:

Conjugation of the Regular Verb *Learn*

Forms of the Verb

Infinite	Base	Present	Present Participle	Past	Past Participle
To learn	learn	learn	learning	learned	(have) learned

Tenses of the Verb

Present Tense

First person:	I learn	we learn
Second person:	you learn	you learn
Third person:	he, she, it learns	they learn

Past Tense

First person:	I learned	we learned
Second person:	you learned	you learned
Third person:	he, she, it learned	they learned

Future Tense (*will* or *shall* + the present)

First person:	I will (shall) learn	we will (shall) learn
Second person:	you will learn	you will learn
Third person:	he, she, it will learn	they will learn

Present Perfect Tense (*have* or *has* + the past participle)

First person:	I have learned	we have learned
Second person:	you have learned	you have learned
Third person:	he, she, it has learned	they have learned

Past Perfect Tense (*had* + the past participle)

First person:	I had learned	we had learned
Second person:	you had learned	you had learned
Third person:	he, she, it had learned	they had learned

Future Perfect Tense (*will have* or *shall have* + the past participle)

First person:	I will (shall) have learned	we will (shall) have learned
Second person:	you will have learned	you will have learned
Third person:	he, she, it will have learned	they will have learned

Rule

Shall or will? Our language is changing. Today, you see *will* used almost always. Shall is used for emphasis—"I *shall* finish my homework" (as if we didn't believe you).

In grammar books published before the 1970s, the distinction is much more formal. When referring to a future event, *shall* is used in the first person, and *will* is used in the second and third persons.

A future event:

First person:	I shall write.	We shall write.
Second person:	You will write.	You will write.
Third person:	He will write.	They will write.

When expressing a determination, command, promise, or threat, will is used in the first person, and shall is used in the second and third persons.

A command:

First person:	I will return.	We will return.
Second person:	You shall return.	You shall return.
Third person:	He shall return.	They shall return.

Progressive Modes of the Verb *Learn*

Present Progressive Mode (*is* or *are* + the present participle)

First person:	I am learning	we are learning
Second person:	you are learning	you are learning
Third person:	he, she, it is learning	they are learning

Past Progressive Mode (*was* or *were* + present participle)

First person:	I was learning	we were learning
Second person:	you were learning	you were learning
Third person:	he, she, it was learning	they were learning

Future Progressive Mode (*will be* or *shall be* + present participle)

First person:	I will be learning	we will be learning
Second person:	you will be learning	you will be learning
Third person:	he, she, it will be learning	they will be learning

Present Perfect Progressive Mode (*has been* or *have been* + present participle)

First person:	I have been learning	we have been learning
Second person:	you have been learning	you have been learning
Third person:	he, she, it has been learning	they have been learning

Past Perfect Progressive Mode (*had been* + present participle)

First person:	I had been learning	we had been learning
Second person:	you had been learning	you had been learning
Third person:	he, she, it had been learning	they had been learning

Future Perfect Progressive Mode (*will have been* + present participle)

First person:	I will have been learning	we will have been learning
Second person:	you will have been learning	you will have been learning
Third person:	he, she, it will have been learning	they will have been learning

The following table is a conjugation of the irregular verb *write*.

Conjugation of the Irregular Verb *Write*

Forms of the Verb

Infinite	Base	Present	Present Participle	Past	Past Participle
To write	write	write	writing	wrote	(have) written

Tenses of the Verb

Present Tense

First person:	I write	we write
Second person:	you write	you write
Third person:	he, she, it writes	they write

Past Tense

First person:	I wrote	we wrote
Second person:	you wrote	you wrote
Third person:	he, she, it wrote	they wrote

Future Tense (*will* or *shall* + the present)

First person:	I will (shall) write	we will (shall) write
Second person:	you will write	you will write
Third person:	he, she it will write	they will write

Present Perfect Tense (*have* or *has* + the past participle)

First person:	I have written	we have written
Second person:	you have written	you have written
Third person:	he, she, it has written	they have written

Past Perfect Tense (*had* + the past participle)

First person:	I had written	we had written
Second person:	you had written	you had written
Third person:	he, she, it had written	they had written

Future Perfect Tense (*will have* or *shall have* + the past participle)

First person:	I will (shall) have written	we will (shall) have written
Second person:	you will have written	you will have written
Third person:	he, she, it will have written	they will have written

Progressive Modes of the Verb *Write*

Present Progressive Mode (*is* or *are* + the present participle)

First person:	I am writing	we are writing
Second person:	you are writing	you are writing
Third person:	he, she, it is writing	they are writing

Past Progressive Mode (*was* or *were* + present participle)

First person:	I was writing	we were writing
Second person:	you were writing	you were writing
Third person:	he, she, it was writing	they were writing

Future progressive mode (*will be* or *shall be* + present participle)

First person:	I will be writing	we will be writing
Second person:	you will be writing	you will be writing
Third person:	he, she, it will be writing	they will be writing

Present Perfect Progressive Mode (*has been* or *have been* + present participle)

First person:	I have been writing	we have been writing
Second person:	you have been writing	you have been writing
Third person:	he, she, it has been writing	they have been writing

Past Perfect Progressive Mode (*had been* + present participle)

First person:	I had been writing	we had been writing
Second person:	you had been writing	you had been writing
Third person:	he, she, it had been writing	they had been writing

Future Perfect Progressive Mode (*will have been* + present participle)

First person:	I will have been writing	we will have been writing
Second person:	you will have been writing	you will have been writing
Third person:	he, she, it will have been writing	they will have been writing

Perfect and Progressive Modes

Intuitively we know that events are more complicated than simply in the past, future, or present. For example, events can start in the past and continue to the moment or they can start before another event in the past. The following guidelines help summarize how verb forms are combined to form tenses and modes referring to specific times:

- A **perfect** mode of a verb uses a form of *have* (*has, have, had*) as a helping verb and a past participle to express an action that is completed or needs to be completed.

- A **progressive** mode of the verb uses a form of *to be* (*is, am, was, were*) as a helping verb and a present participle to express an action that is or was happening.

- The **progressive and perfect modes combined** use a form of *have*, a form of *to be*, and a participle to express an action that relates to some future action.

Guidelines for When to Use What Tense or Mode

Use the *present tense* for the following:

- Stating a fact (or a universal truth)

  The earth *revolves* around the sun.

  My grandchild *is* three years old.

  Jim *swims* every morning.

  They *sing* in the festival.

  The owl *perches* in the tree outside my window.

- Indicating an action occurring at the present time (or a condition existing now)

  My parents *own* a llama.

  The llama *is* very young.

  She *works* at the house.

  The house *is* on fire.

  I *hear* the fire truck.

- Presenting a generalization (an assertion of opinion)

  My grandchild *is* brilliant.

  That store *overcharges* its customers.

  That restaurant *makes* the best soup.

  Hot water *works* better than cold for curing a cold.

  The small ones *are* the best.

Use the *past tense* for the following:

- An action that occurred in the past (or a condition that existed in the past).

  The team *finished* the project.

  They *published* the book.

  Samantha *walked* the dog.

  I *completed* my homework.

  He *ate* the entire meal.

Use the *future tense* (*shall* or *will* + present tense) for the following:

■ An action that will occur in the future (or a condition that will exist in the future).

I *will be* at the game tomorrow.

I *shall finish* my homework.

Tony *will pick up* the groceries.

The barbeque *will be* at the park.

The ceremony *shall start* on time.

Use the *present perfect* tense (*has* or *have* + past participle) for the following:

■ A past action that has occurred continuously up to the present and still continues.
■ A past action that has been repeated.

The college *has been* operating for over 100 years.

It *has been* hot this spring.

He *has taken* the vitamins every day.

They *have attended* all of the workshops.

The trainers *have worked* with the dogs.

Use the *past perfect* tense (*had* + past participle) for the following:

■ A past action completed before another past action.

We *had drunk* our tea before the crumpets arrived.

They *had studied* for three hours when they realized the test was not until next week.

I *had reviewed* the material all weekend before taking the test.

She *had broken* all the records before winning the title.

He *had written* several novels by the time he was discovered by a literary agent.

Use the *future perfect* tense (*will have* or *shall have* + past participle) for the following:

■ An action that needs to be completed before another future action.

We *will have passed* all the qualifying tests before the end of the year.

They *will have danced* for 24 hours by the time this event is finished tomorrow.

He *will have set up* the displays before the customers arrive.

It *will have run* for 10 hours by the time we arrive.

The triathletes *will have run* the race before they bike.

Use the *present progressive* mode (*is* or *are* + present participle) for the following:

■ An action in progress.

The ship *is sailing* in the bay.

The hippos *are missing*.

The elephants *are training* for the event.

The cowboy *is riding* into town.

The students *are learning* about verbs.

Use the *past progressive* mode (*was* or *were* + present participle) for the following:

■ An action happening when another action in the past is happening.

The ship *was sailing* in the bay when the hurricane struck.

The elephants *were walking* through the circus tent when hippos disappeared.

The bird *was flying* when the hunter shot.

He *was acting* in the play as we watched.

Use the *future progressive* mode (*will be* or *shall be* + present participle) for the following:

■ An action that will take place in the future.

He *will be receiving* the delivery at noon.

The governor *shall be receiving* the complaint by Friday.

The tiger *will be arriving* by freight.

Pat *shall be greeting* the dignitaries as they arrive.

The birds *will be returning* to the wildlife refuge in the spring.

Remember from the definitions above that a **perfect** mode of a verb uses a form of *have* (has, have, had) as a helping verb and a past participle to express a completed action. A **progressive** mode of the verb uses a form of *be* (*is, am, was, were*) as a helping verb and a present participle to express an action that is or was happening. Therefore, a perfect progressive mode together contains a form of *have*, a form of *be*, and a participle, as outlined below.

Use the *present perfect progressive* mode (*has been* or *have been* + present participle) for the following:

■ An action happening in the past.

The children *have been participating* in the annual event.

Anne *has been writing* everyday.

Bob *has been singing* in the choir.

The water *has been running* in the grass.

They *have been returning* to the cabin.

Use the *past perfect progressive* mode (*had been* + present participle) for the following:

- An action happening in the past before another past action.

  The miners *had been digging* for days before they struck gold.

  His fever *had been rising* all night before he took the antibiotic.

  She *had been asking* for service when the waitress arrived.

  The hippos *had been roaming* the city when the police found them.

Use the *future perfect progressive* mode (*will have been* + present participle) for the following:

- An action that will happen in the future at the same time as another action.

  He *will have been driving* throughout the night when the route is finished.

  The water *will have been running* in the grass all afternoon by the time we return to turn it off.

  They *will have been returning* to the cabin for 10 years when the work is finally completed.

  Sara *will have been studying* for 10 years when she finishes her medical specialty.

  The ground *will have been* covered with snow by the time we decide to mow.

Appendix

Answers to the Practice Questions

PRACTICE 1–1

1. noun

2. pronouns

3. verbs

4. adjective

5. articles

6. adverb

7. prepositions

1.

2.

3.

4.

5.

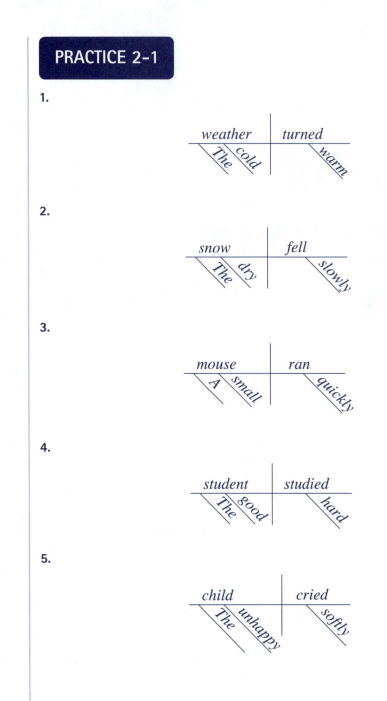

1.

2.

3.

4.

5.

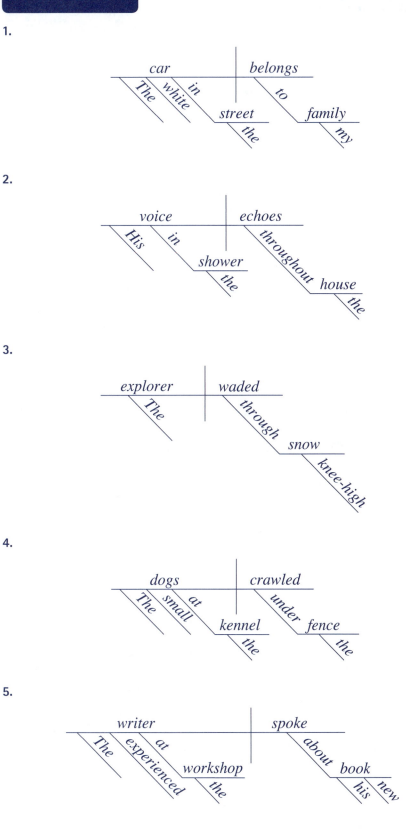

PRACTICE 2-3

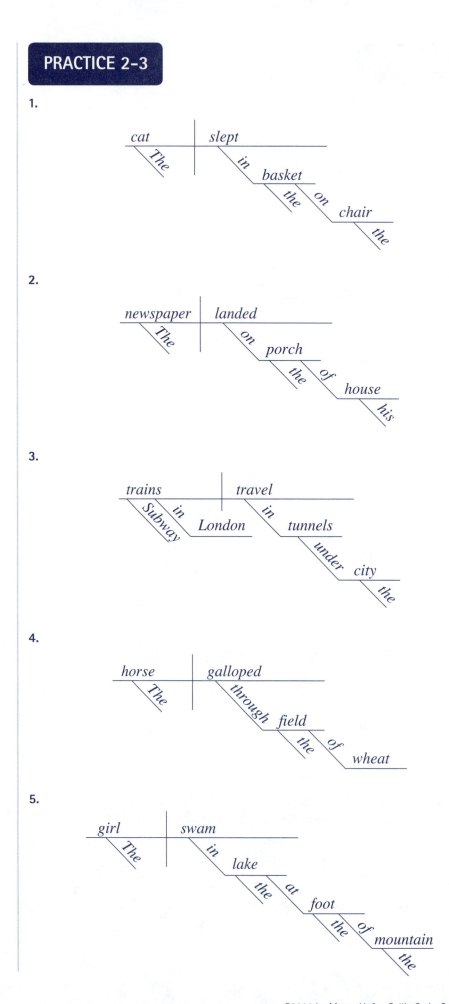

1.

2.

3.

4.

5.

PRACTICE 2-4

1.

2.

3.

4.

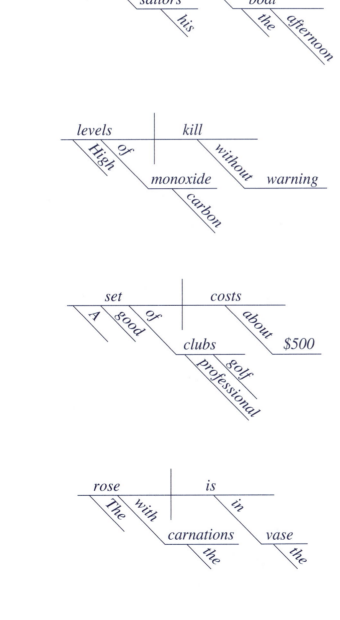

5.

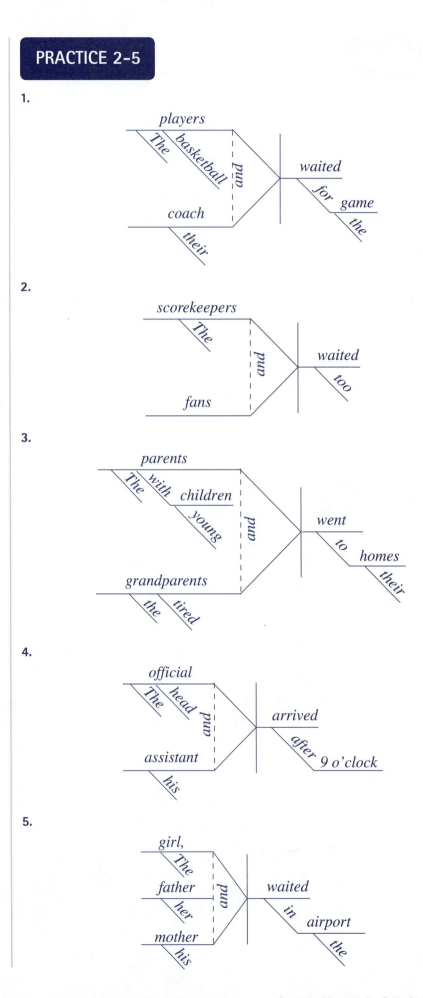

PRACTICE 2-5

1.

players
The basketball and
coach their
waited
for game
the

2.

scorekeepers
The and
fans
waited
too

3.

parents
The with children
young
and
grandparents
the tired
went
to homes
their

4.

official
The head and
assistant
his
arrived
after 9 o'clock

5.

girl,
The and
father
her
mother
his
waited
in airport
the

130

PRACTICE 2-6

1.

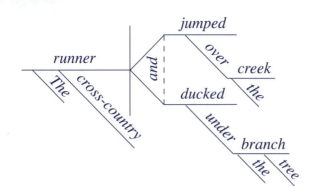

2.

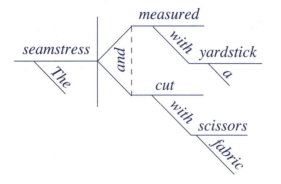

3.

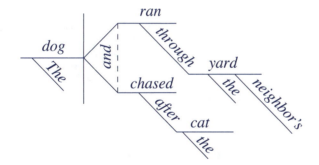

4.

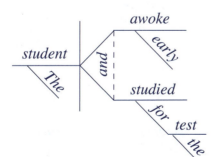

5.

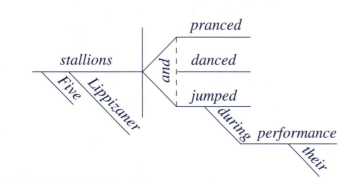

PRACTICE 2-7

1.

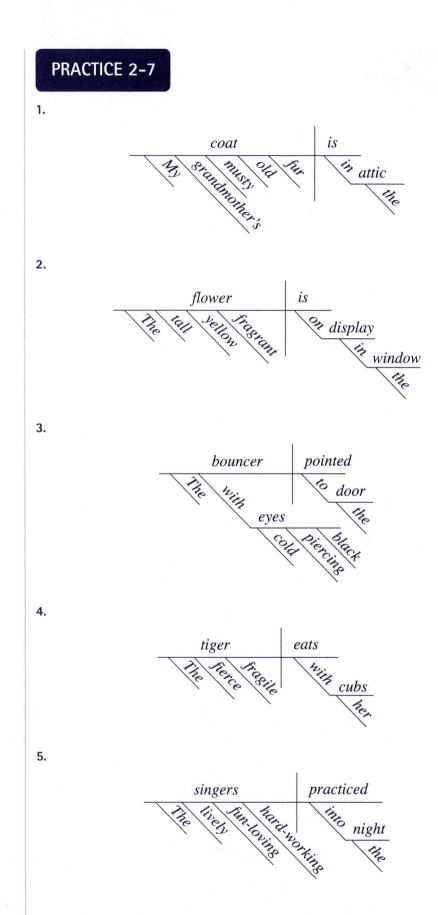

2.

3.

4.

5.

PRACTICE 2-8

1.

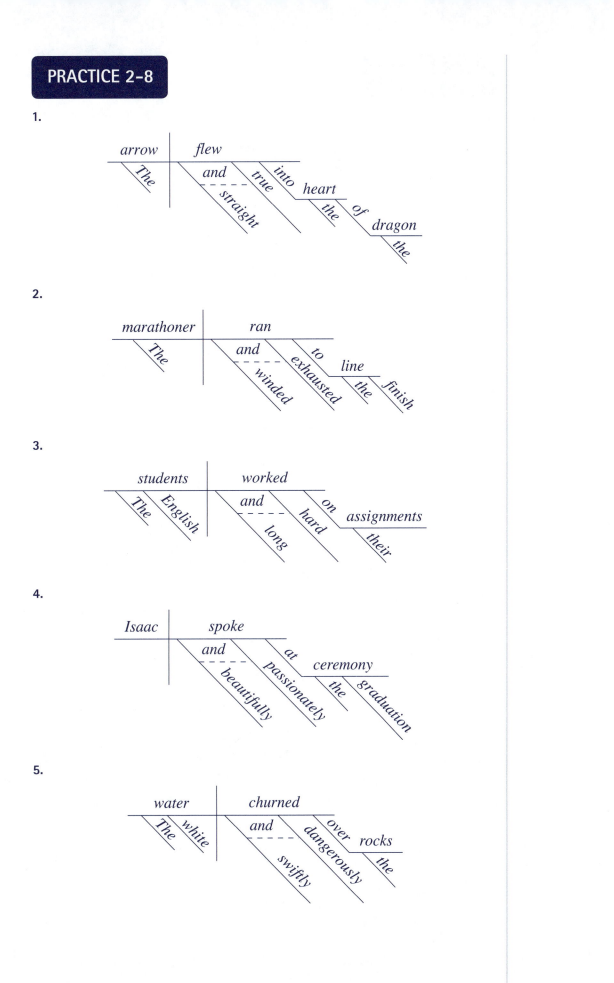

2.

3.

4.

5.

1.

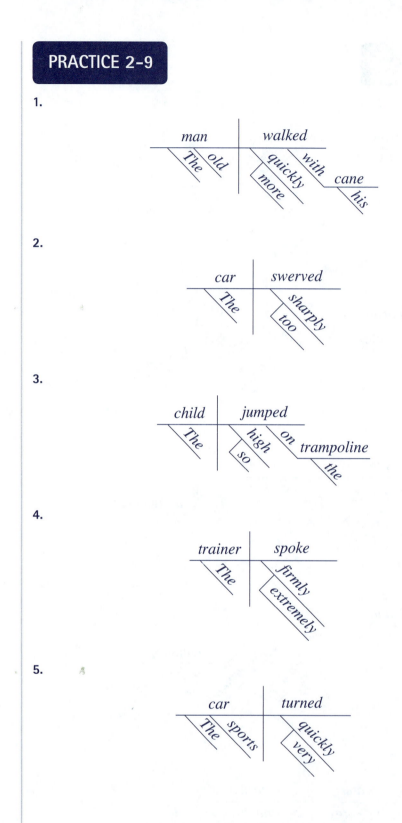

man / walked
The old / quickly more / with cane his

2.

car / swerved
The / sharply too

3.

child / jumped
The / high so / on trampoline the

4.

trainer / spoke
The / firmly extremely

5.

car / turned
The sports / quickly very

PRACTICE 2-10

1.

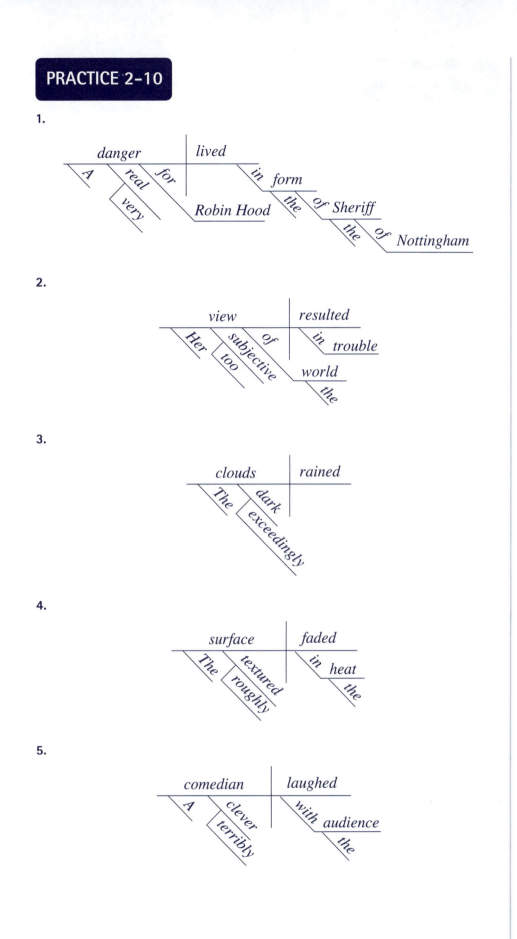

2.

3.

4.

5.

1.

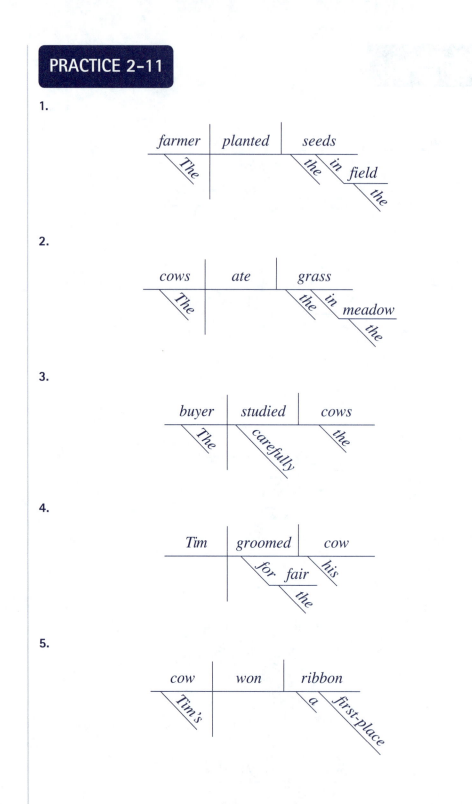

farmer | planted | seeds
The | | the | in field | the

2.

cows | ate | grass
The | | the | in meadow | the

3.

buyer | studied | cows
The | carefully | the

4.

Tim | groomed | cow
for fair | his | the

5.

cow | won | ribbon
Tim's | a | first-place

1.

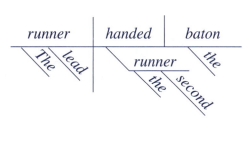

2.

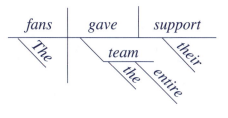

3.

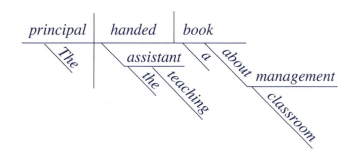

4.

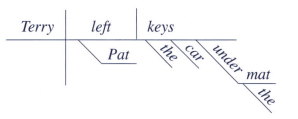

5.

1.

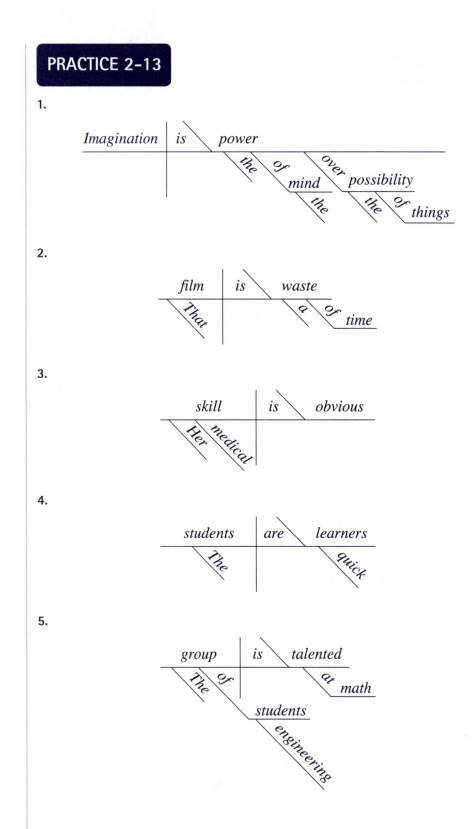

Imagination | is \ power
the / of / mind / over / possibility
the / the / of / things

2.

film | is \ waste
That / a \ of / time

3.

skill | is \ obvious
Her / medical

4.

students | are \ learners
The / quick

5.

group | is \ talented
The / of / students / at / math
engineering

1.

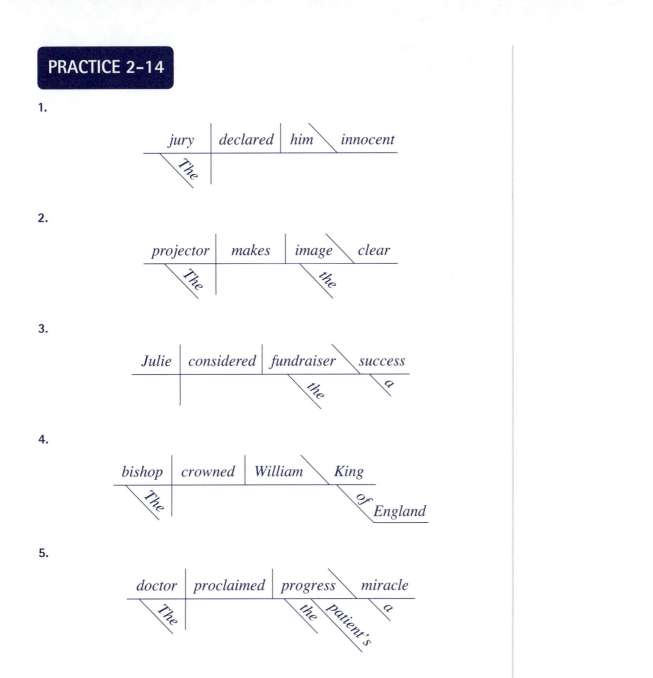

jury | declared | him \ innocent
The

2.

projector | makes | image \ clear
The | | the

3.

Julie | considered | fundraiser \ success
the | a

4.

bishop | crowned | William \ King
The | of England

5.

doctor | proclaimed | progress \ miracle
The | the | patient's | a

1.

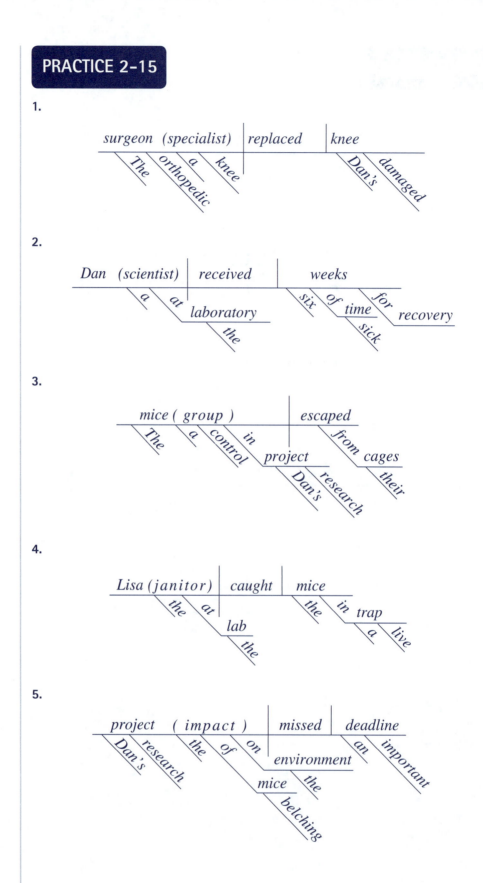

2.

3.

4.

5.

1.

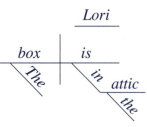

2.

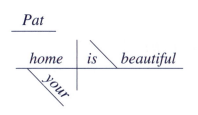

3.

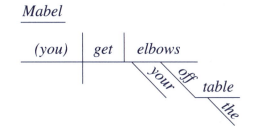

4.

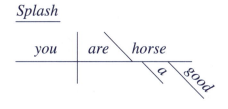

5.

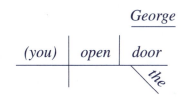

COMPREHENSIVE PRACTICE 2-17

1.

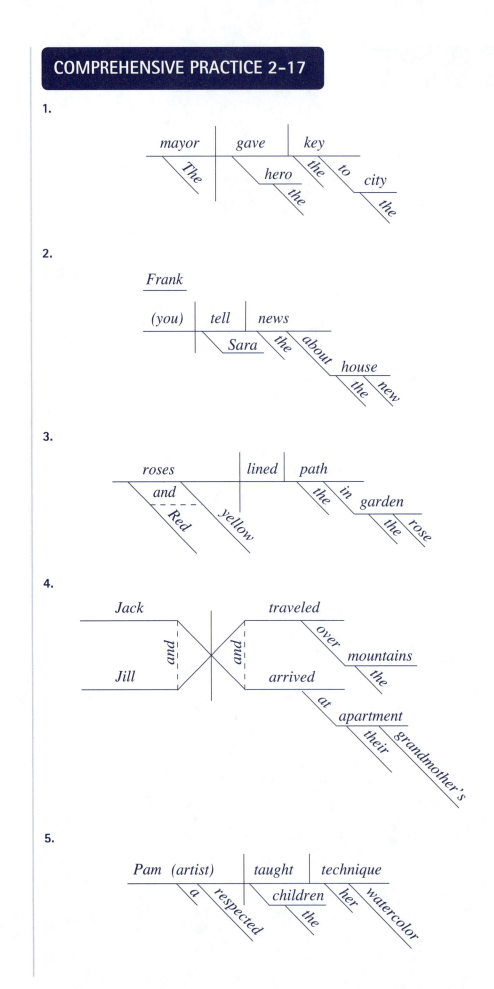

2.

3.

4.

5.

6.

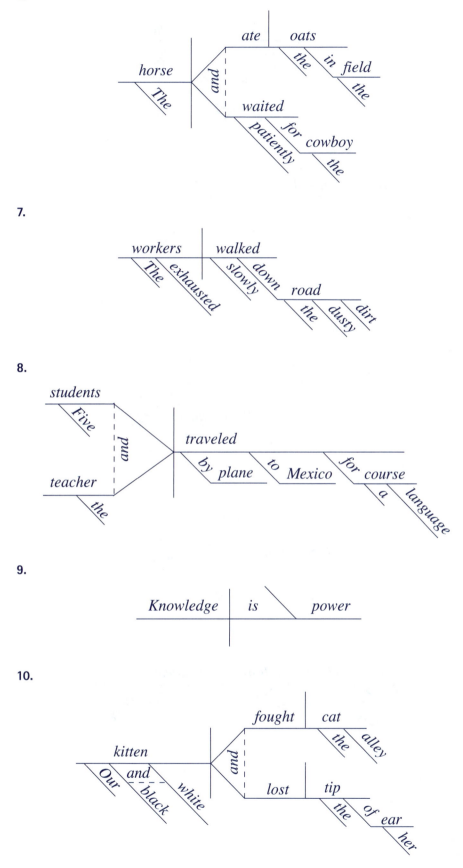

7.

8.

9.

10.

11.

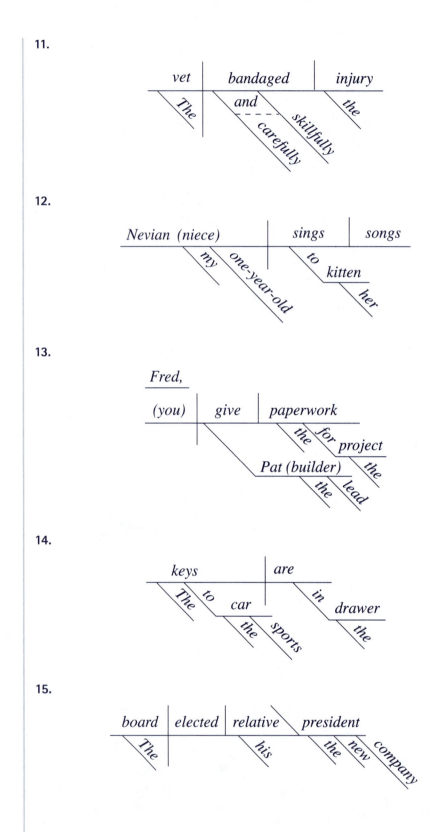

vet | bandaged | injury
The | and | the
skillfully
carefully

12.

Nevian (niece) | sings | songs
my | one-year-old | to kitten
her

13.

Fred,

(you) | give | paperwork
the | for project
Pat (builder) | the
the | lead

14.

keys | are
The | to car | in drawer
the | sports | the

15.

board | elected | relative \ president
The | his | the new company

16.

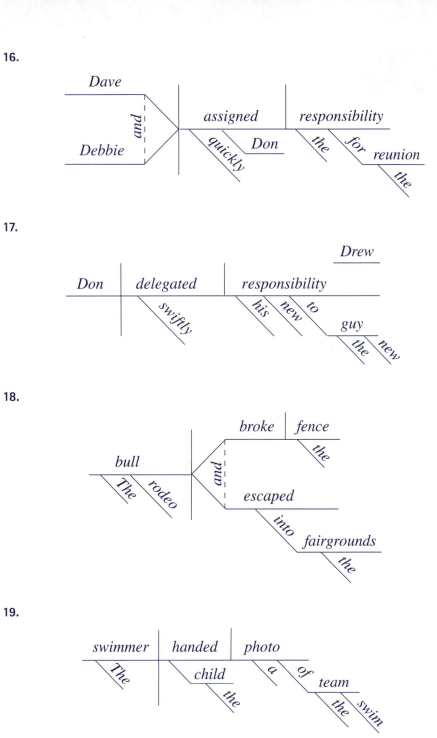

17.

18.

19.

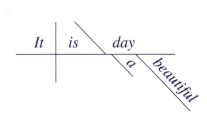

20.

1.

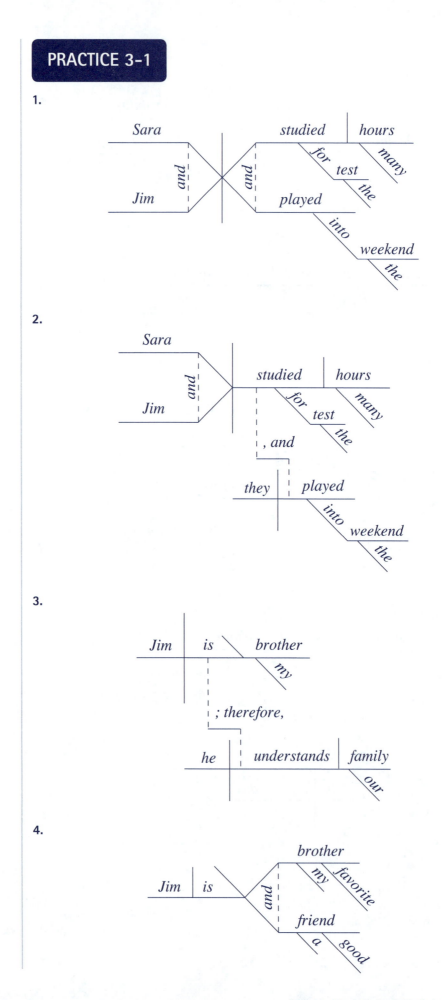

2.

3.

4.

5.

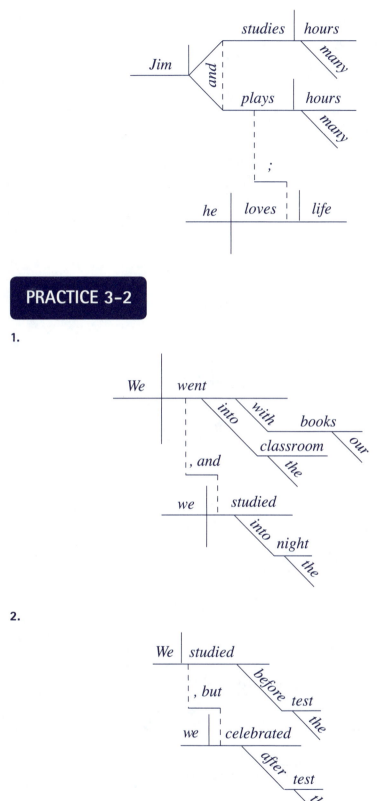

PRACTICE 3-2

1.

2.

3.

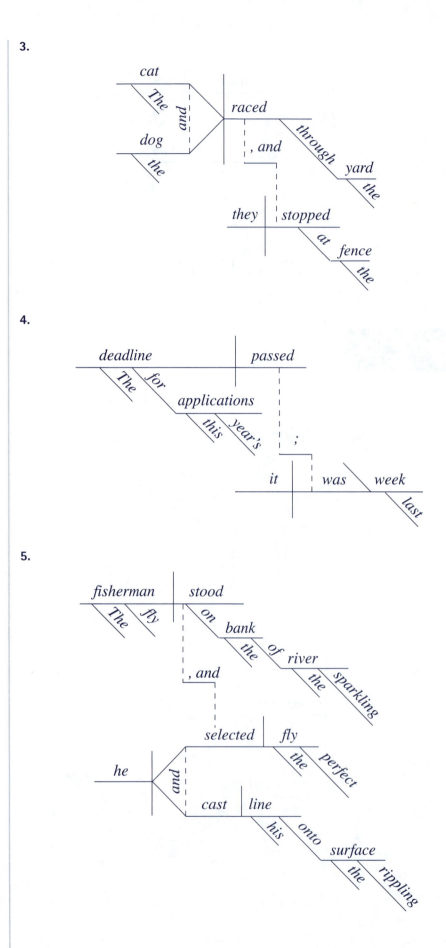

4.

5.

COMPREHENSIVE PRACTICE 3-3

1.

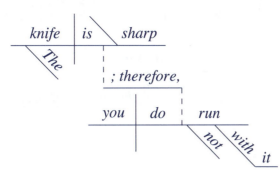

2.

3.

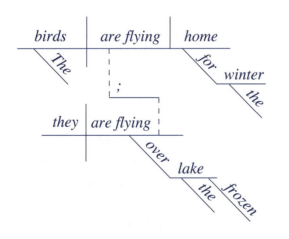

4.

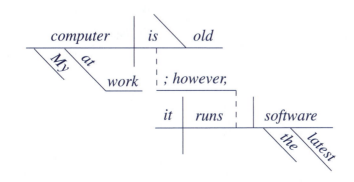

5.

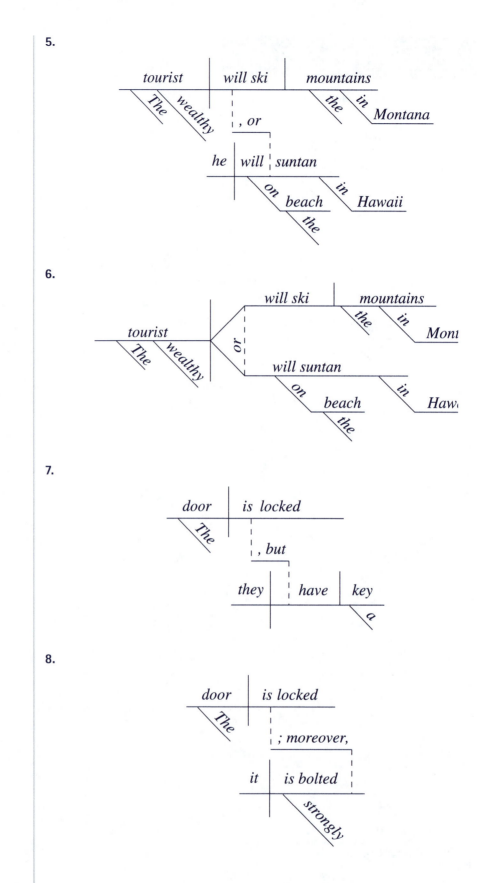

6.

7.

8.

9.

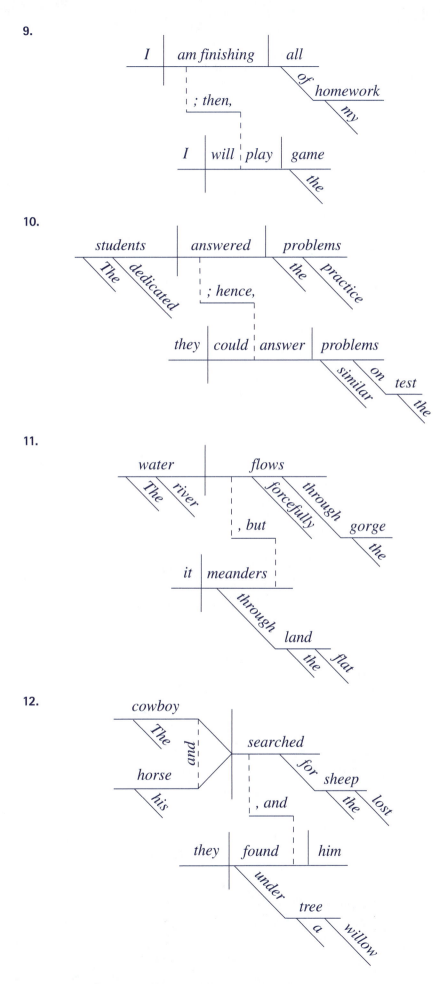

10.

11.

12.

13.

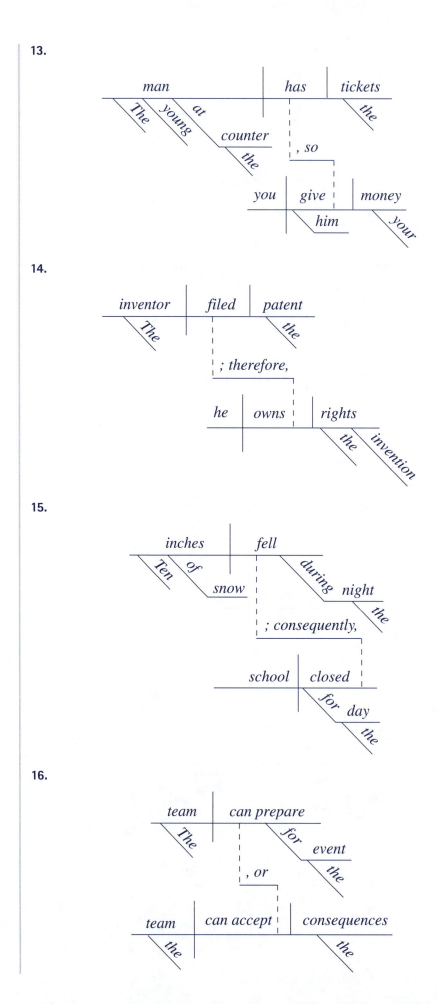

14.

15.

16.

17.

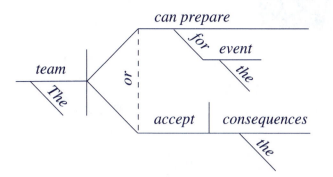

18.

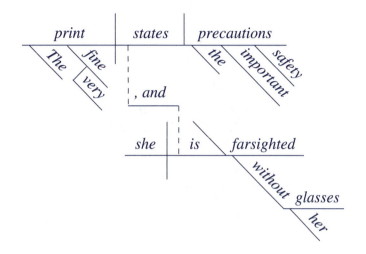

19.

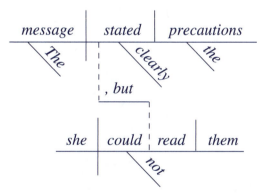

20.

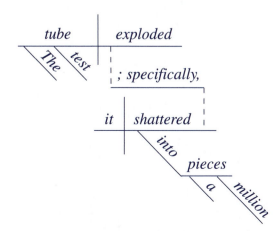

PRACTICE 4-1

1.

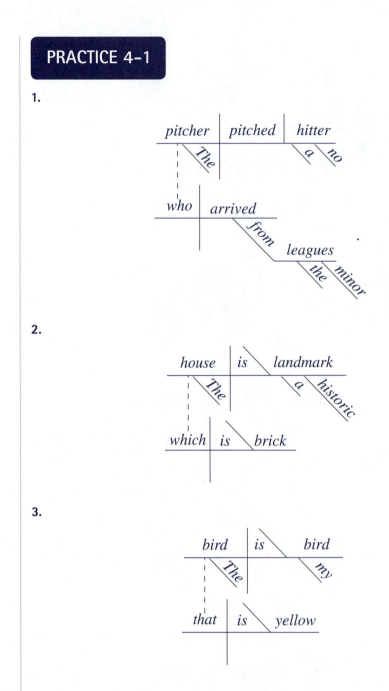

2.

3.

1.

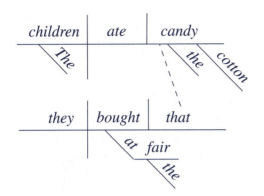

2.

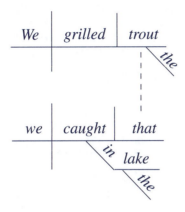

3.

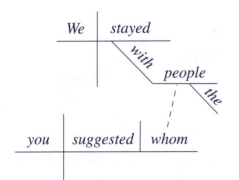

1.

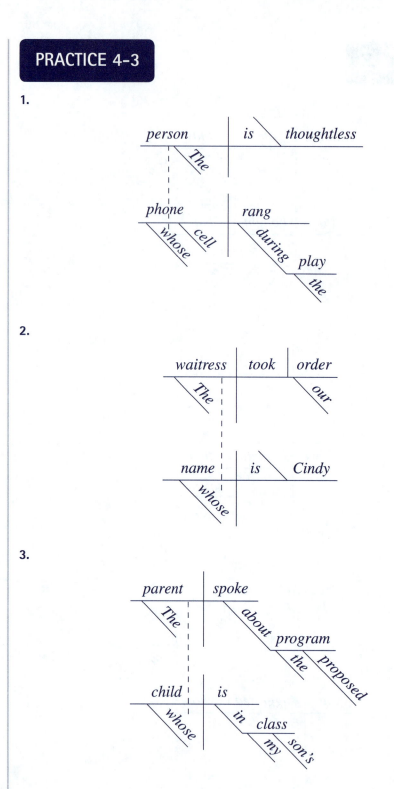

2.

3.

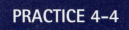

1.

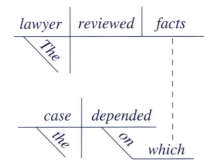

2.

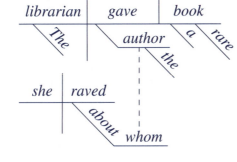

3.

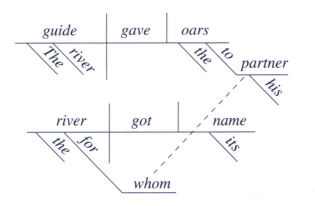

PRACTICE 4-5

1.

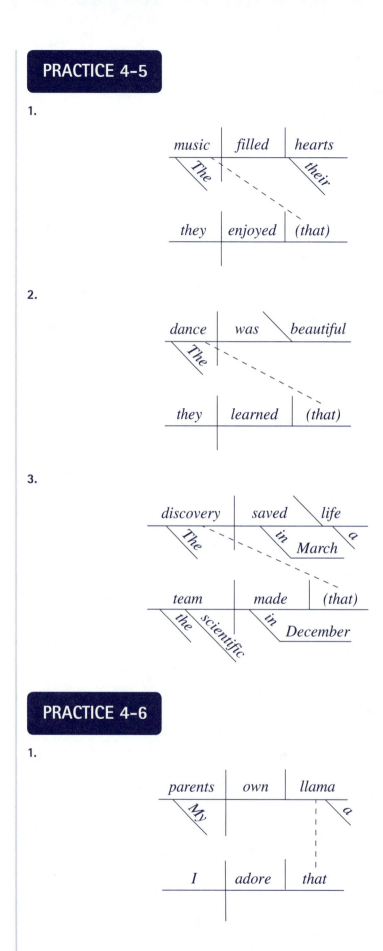

2.

3.

PRACTICE 4-6

1.

2.

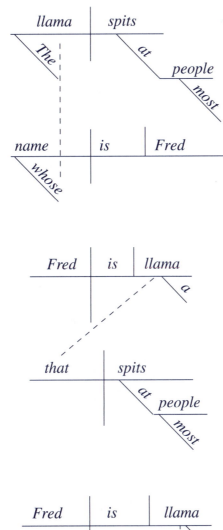

3.

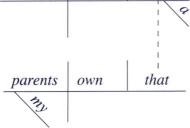

4.

5.

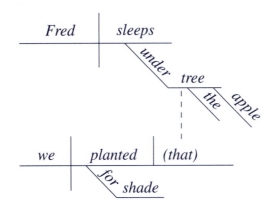

PRACTICE 4-7

1.

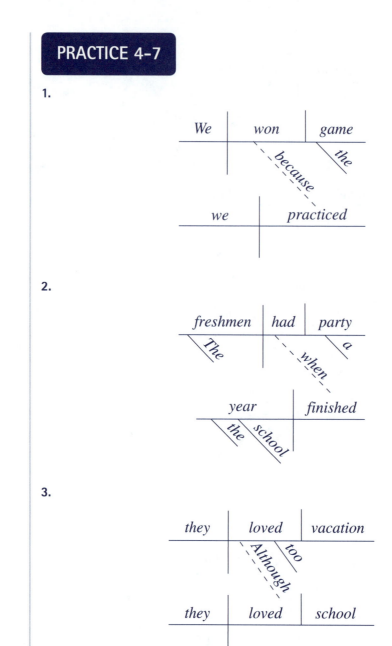

2.

3.

PRACTICE 4-8

1.

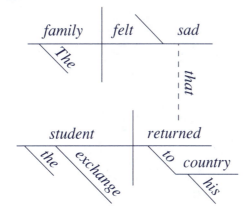

2.

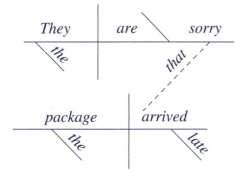

3.

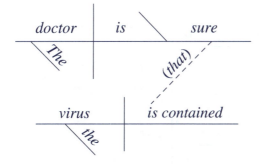

PRACTICE 4-9

1.

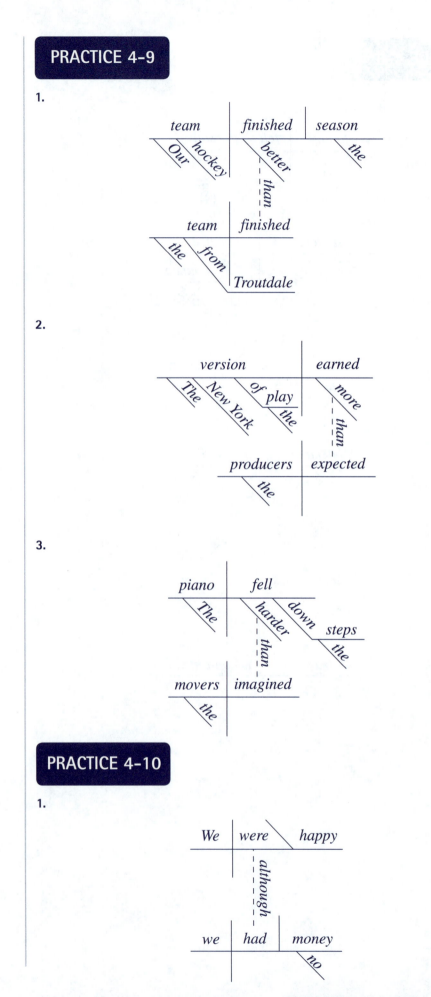

2.

3.

PRACTICE 4-10

1.

2.

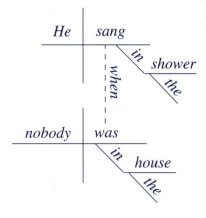

3.

2.

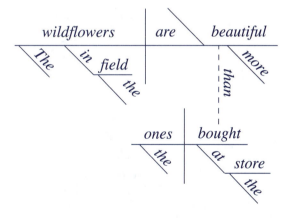

3.

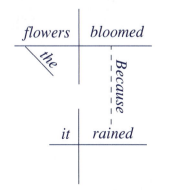

1.

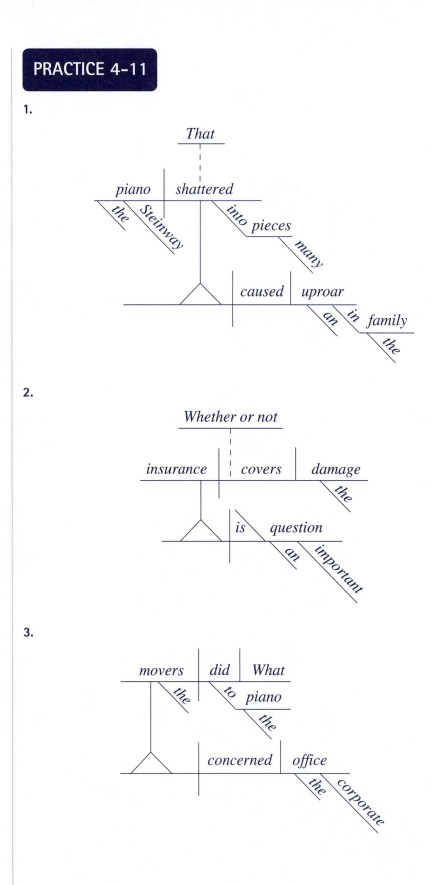

2.

3.

1.

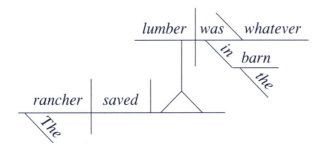

2.

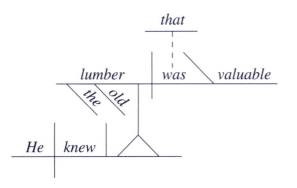

3.

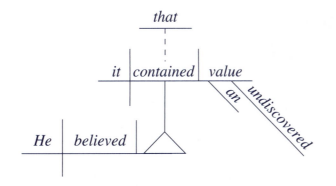

PRACTICE 4–13

1.

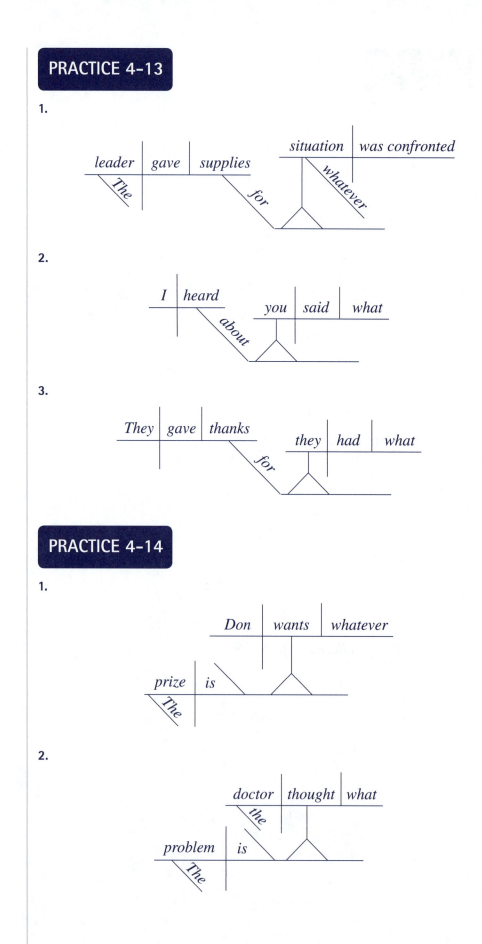

2.

3.

PRACTICE 4–14

1.

2.

3.

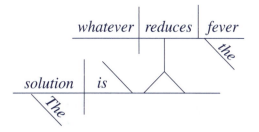

COMPREHENSIVE PRACTICE 4-15

1.

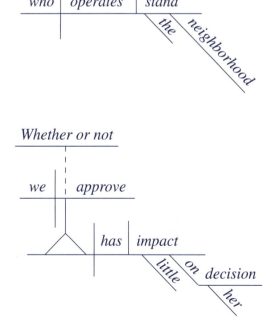

2.

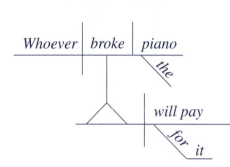

3.

4.

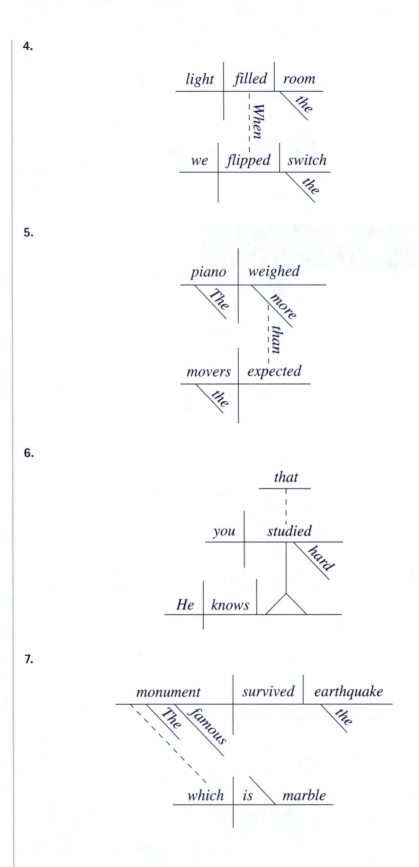

5.

6.

7.

8.

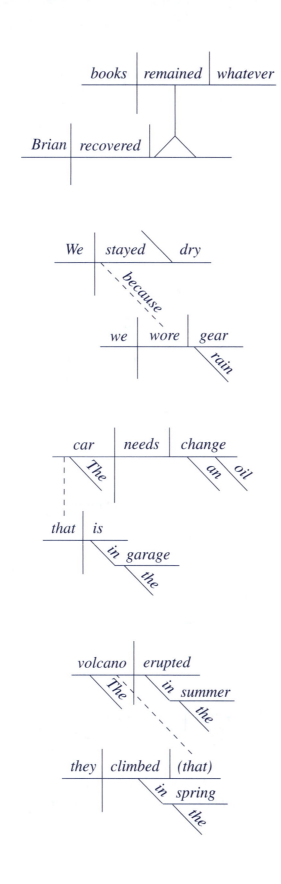

books | remained | whatever

Brian | recovered

9.

We | stayed \ dry

because

we | wore | gear

rain

10.

car | needs | change

The

an \ oil

that | is

in garage

the

11.

volcano | erupted

The

in summer

the

they | climbed | (that)

in spring

the

12.

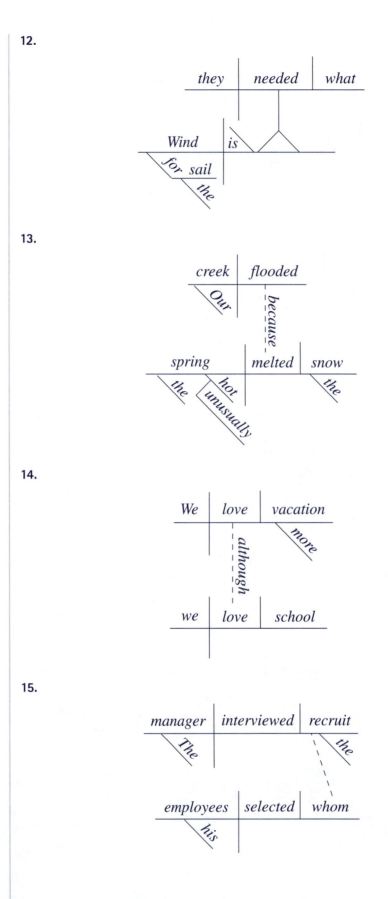

13.

14.

15.

16.

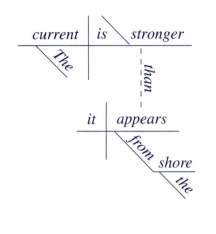

17.

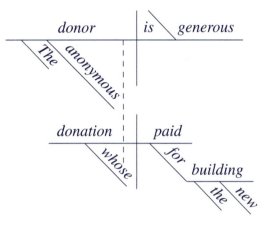

18.

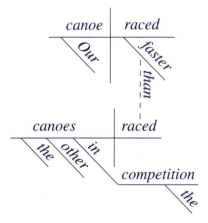

19.

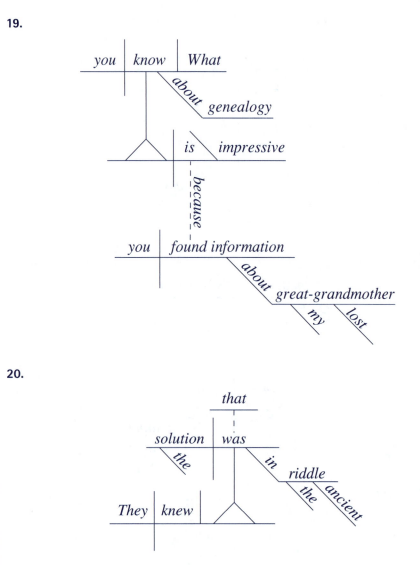

20.

PRACTICE 5-1

1.

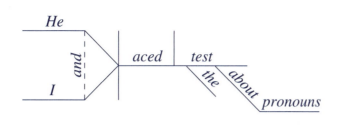

2.

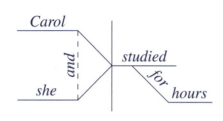

3.

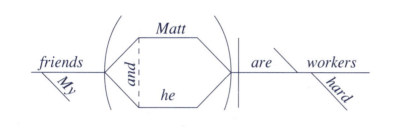

4.

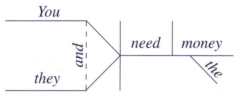

5.

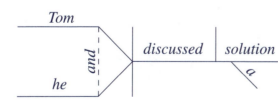

1.

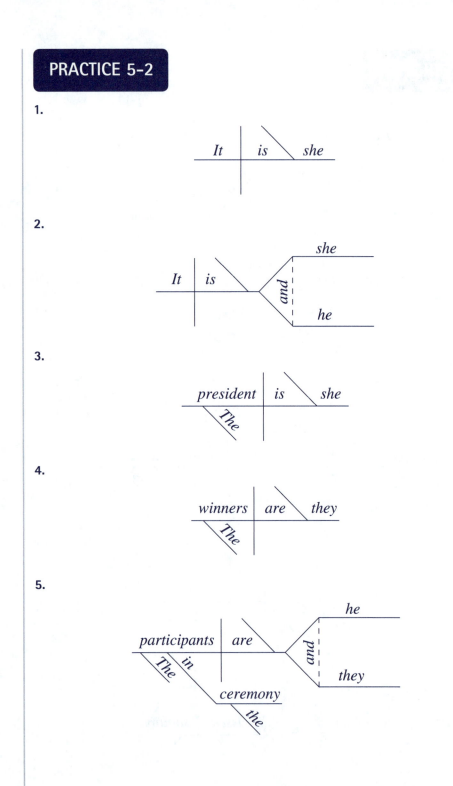

2.

3.

4.

5.

PRACTICE 5-3

1.

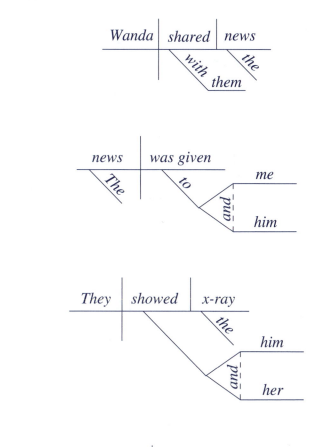

Wanda | shared | news
with them
the

2.

news | was given
The
to
me
and
him

3.

They | showed | x-ray
the
him
and
her

4.

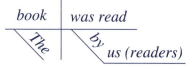

book | was read
The
by us (readers)

5.

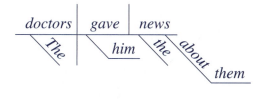

doctors | gave | news
The
him
the
about them

PRACTICE 5-4

1.

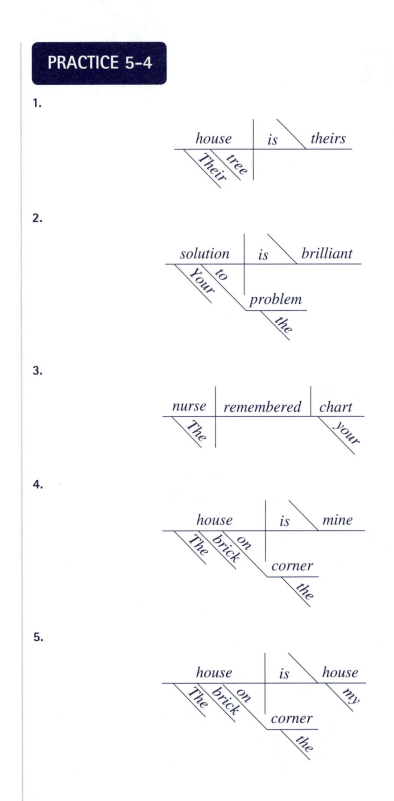

2.

3.

4.

5.

1.

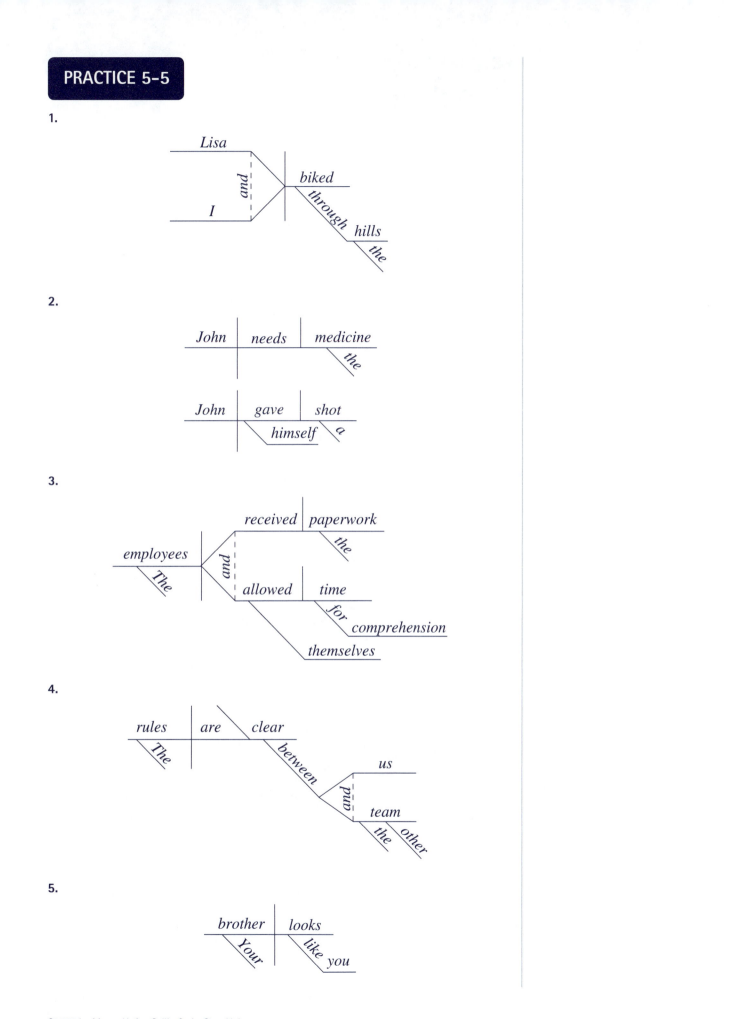

2.

3.

4.

5.

1.

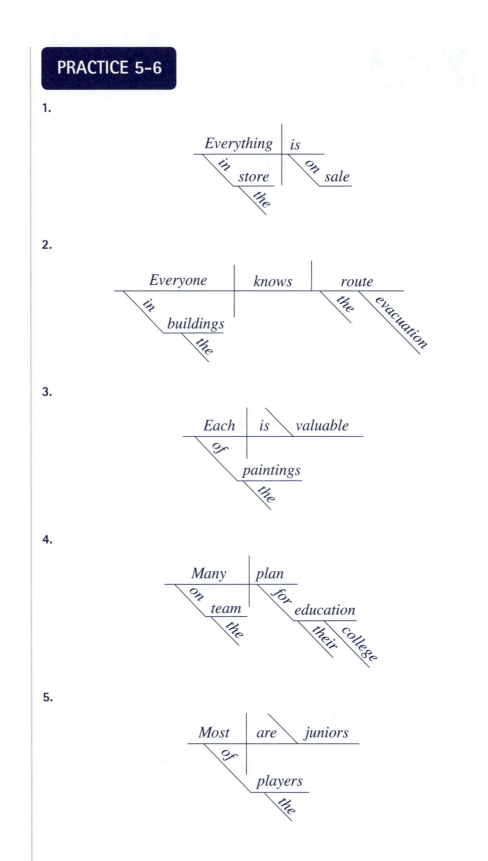

2.

3.

4.

5.

COMPREHENSIVE PRACTICE 5–7

1.

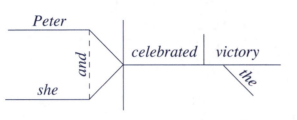

2.

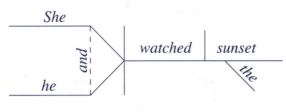

3.

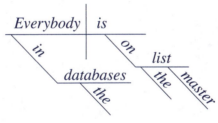

4.

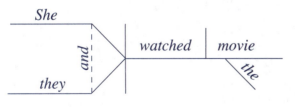

5.

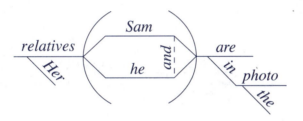

6.

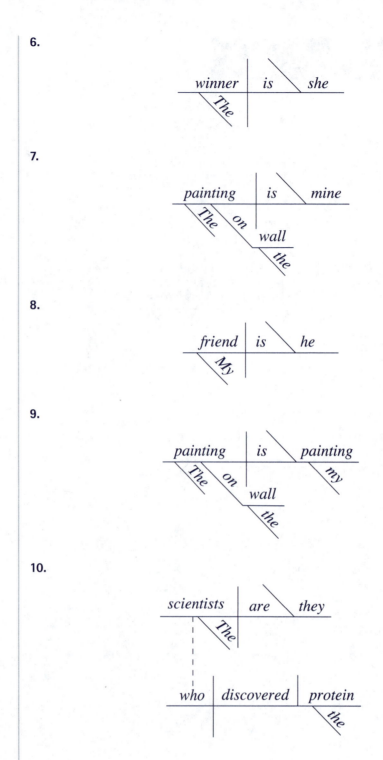

7.

8.

9.

10.

11.

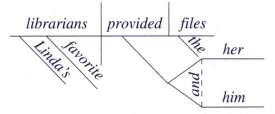
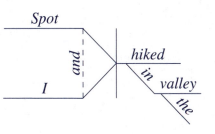

12.

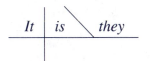
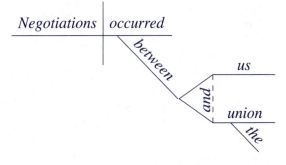
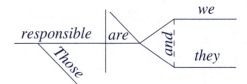

13.

It | is \ they

14.

Negotiations | occurred
between
and
us
union
the

15.

responsible | are
Those
and
we
they

16.

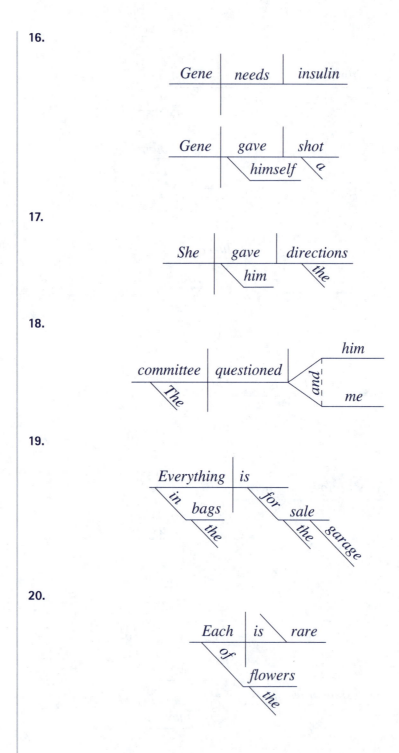

17.

18.

19.

20.

PRACTICE 6-1

1.

seal | is \ comfortable
A
swimming
in sea
the cold

2.

driver | missed | exit
the young the
Focusing
on road
the

3.

teacher | praised | students
the the
Thrilled
by work
their

4.

horse | caused | commotion
The a
galloping
through Main Street

5.

signs | provide | names
The the of flowers
located
throughout garden
the city

PRACTICE 6-2

1.

2.

3.

4.

5.

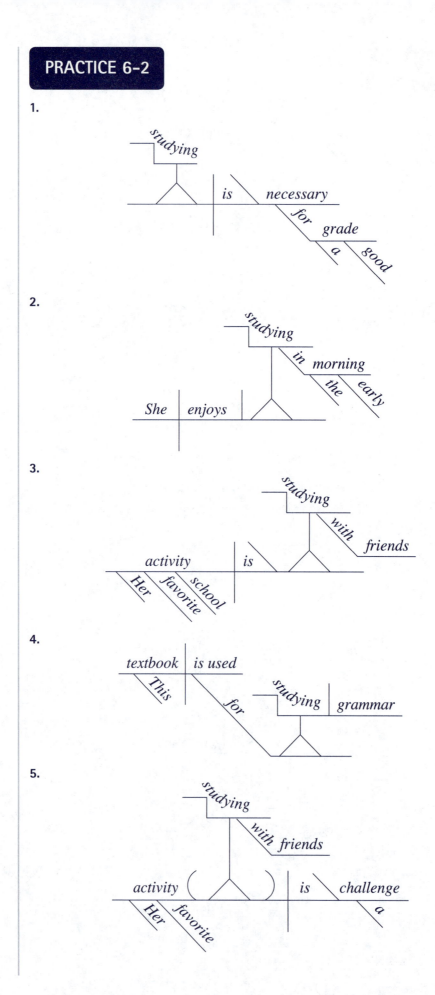

©2008 by Marye Hefty, Sallie Ortiz, Sara Nelson

1.

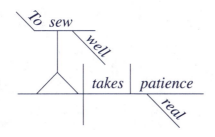

2.

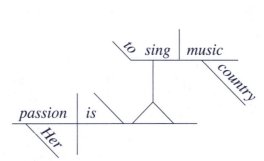

3.

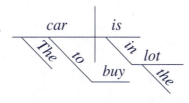

4.

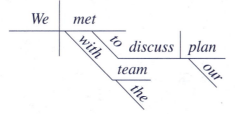

5.

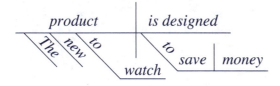

1.

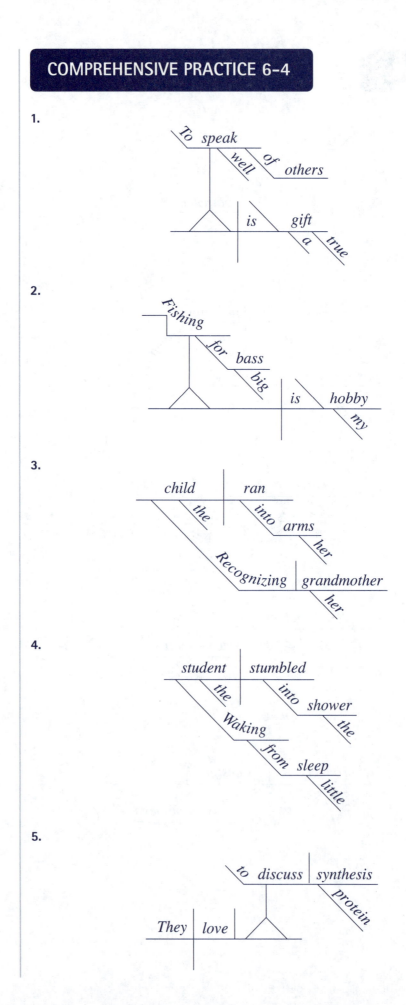

2.

3.

4.

5.

6.

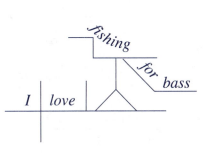

7.

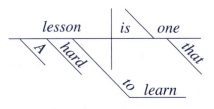

8.

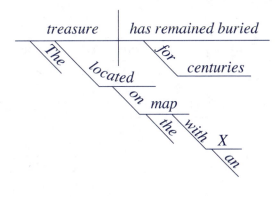

9.

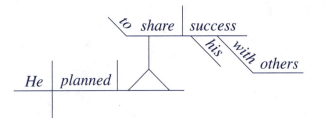

10.

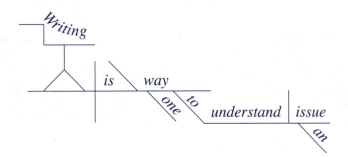

11.

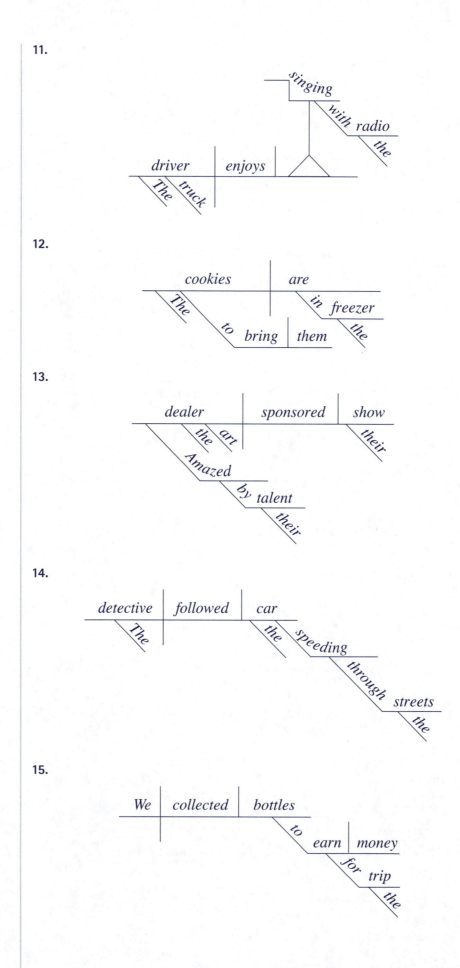

12.

13.

14.

15.

16.

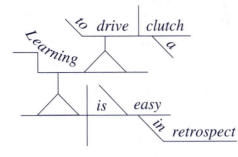

17.

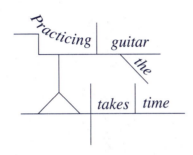

18.

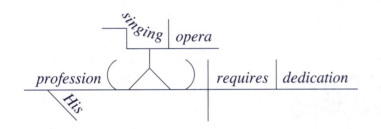

19.

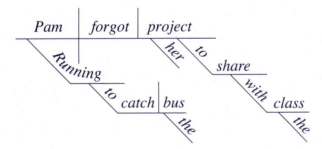

20.

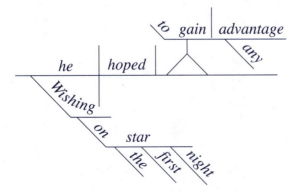

1. enjoys

2. love

3. reads

4. study

5. diagrams

6. learns

7. learn

8. floats

9. select

10. take

1. imperative	watch
2. indicative	was
3. subjunctive	were, were
4. subjunctive	be
5. indicative	is
6. imperative	turn
7. indicative	are
8. subjunctive	be
9. subjunctive	were
10. subjunctive	be taken

Index

A

Adjective 2

adjective clause 46–54

    diagramming adjective clauses 48–54

multiple adjectives 17

    comma rule 18

Adverb 2

adverb clause 54–59

    diagramming adverb clauses 55–59

    identifying adverb clauses 55

    punctuation of adverb clauses 59

    rule for omitting the word "that" 57

coordinating conjunctions for adverb clauses 54

conjunctive adverbs 38

list of commonly used conjunctive adverbs 38

Appositives 33

appositive phrases 33

nouns of address 33

Antecedent 46

Article 2

Auxiliary (helping) verbs 103–105

B

"Be" or "to be" verbs 102

C

Comma splice 43

Complex sentence 45–68

dependent and independent clauses 45

Compound sentence 37–44

diagramming compound sentences 39

independent clause 37

    types of independent clauses 45

        adjective clause 46–54

        adverb clause 54

        noun clause 61

punctuation for compound sentences 38

Conjunction 3

subordinating conjunction 54

D

Diagramming

adjective 7

    adjective clause 48

        with a relative pronoun that functions as a subject 49

        as a direct object 49

        as an adjective 50

        as an object of a preposition 51

        with an omitted but understood relative pronoun 52

adverbs 7

    adverb clauses 54–59

        that modifies a verb 54

        an adjective 56

        an adverb 58

appositives 33

    appositive phrases 33

compound sentences 39

    joined with a semicolon 39

    joined with a coordinating conjunction 40

    joined with a conjunctive adverb preceded by a semicolon and followed by a comma 41

direct objects 24–25

indirect objects 26–27

multiple parts of speech 13–20

    coordinating conjunctions 14

    compound subjects 13–15

    compound verbs 15–17

    compound adjectives 17–19

        commas in multiple adjectives 18–19

multiple adverbs 19–20

    adverbs that modify adjectives 21–22

    adverbs that modify adverbs 20–21

nouns 1

    noun clauses 61–67

        that function as subjects 61

           as direct objects 61

           as the object of a preposition 61

           as subjective complements 62

    nouns of address 34–35

    compound subjects 13

objective complements 32

prepositional phrases 8–11

    adjective prepositional phrases 7

    adverbial prepositional phrases 7

    multiple prepositional phrases 10–11

    prepositional phrases that modify other

        prepositional phrases 11

personal pronouns 69

    subjective case pronouns 71–72

        used for subjective complements 72–73

    objective case pronouns 73–75

    possessive case pronouns 75–77

    reflexive and intensive pronouns 77–78

    indefinite pronouns 78–80

    relative pronouns 81–83

        as a subject 82

        as an adjective 82

        as a direct object 82

        as the object of a preposition 83

        relative pronoun omitted 83

simple sentences 5–36

subjective complements 27

    Linking verbs 23

subject–Verb agreement 12–13

verbals 87–97

    gerunds and gerund phrases 91–93

    infinitive phrases functioning as nouns 93

        as adjectives and adverbs 93

    participles and participle phrases 87–90

verbs 6, 95

    compound verbs 15–16

Direct and indirect objects 23–27

Direct objects 24–25

F

Fragments 60

G

Gerund 90–92

    diagramming gerund and gerund phrases 91–92

I

Indirect Objects 26–27

Independent clause 37

    punctuation of independent clauses:

        semicolon 37

        comma and coordinating conjunction 37

        conjunctive adverb preceded by a semicolon and

           followed by a comma 38

Infinitive 87, 93–95

    infinitives functioning as nouns 93

        as adjectives and adverbs 93

    diagramming infinitive phrases functioning as

        nouns 94

        as adjectives and adverbs 25

Interjection 33

N

Noun 1

    noun clauses 61–66

        diagramming noun clauses 62–66

        distinguishing types of noun clauses 62

        identifying a noun clause 61

    nouns of address 34

    subject 27

        subjective complement 27–28

           identity test (for subjective

             complement) 28–29

           types 29–30

           diagramming 30–31

        predicate nominative 29

    diagramming nouns 6

O

Objective complement 32

P

Participle 87–90

    present participle phrases 88

    past participle phrases 88

diagramming participles and participle
    phrases 88–89

Parts of Speech 1–4

Predicate nominative 29

Predicate adjective 29

Preposition
  definition 2
  list of common prepositions 3
  prepositional phrases 8

Pronouns 1, 69–86
  appositives, appositive phrases 33
  demonstrative pronouns 80
  indefinite Pronouns 78–80
    diagramming indefinite pronouns 79
    list of common indefinite pronouns 79
  interrogative pronouns 85
  personal pronouns 69–72
    subjective case pronouns 71–73
      diagramming subjective case
        pronouns 72–73
        subjective case pronouns used for
          subjective complements 72–73
    objective case pronouns 73–75
      diagramming objective case
        pronouns 73–74
    possessive case pronouns 75–77
      diagramming possessive case
        pronouns 76
  reciprocal pronouns 85–86
  reflexive and intensive pronouns 77–78
    diagramming reflexive and intensive
      pronouns 78
  relative pronouns 82–83
    diagramming relative pronouns 82–83
  who or whom? (understanding when to use) 83–84

Punctuation
  adverb clauses 59
  appositive rule (commas or no commas) 34
  commas in multiple adjectives 18–19
  comma rule 18
  comma splice 43
  compound sentences 37
    joined with a semicolon 37
    joined with a coordinating conjunction 37–38

    joined with a conjunctive adverb preceded
      by a semicolon and followed by a
      comma 38
  independent clauses 37–38
    comma and coordinating conjunction 37
    conjunctive adverb preceded by a semicolon and
      followed by a comma 38
    semicolon 37

R

Rules
  antecedents 47
  appositives rule (commas or no commas) 34
  commas in multiple adjectives rule 18–19
  omitting the word "that" in an adverb clause 57
  pronoun rules:
    pronouns used as appositives or in appositive
      phrases 34
    possessive case pronouns 76
    relative pronouns (when to use that, which,
      who, whom, or whose with specific
      antecedents) 81
    understanding when to use who and whom 83–84
  punctuation rules for adverb clauses 59
  punctuation for compound sentences 38–39
  subject–Verb agreement rule 12
  verb "be" or "to be" rule 102
  verb tenses "Shall" or "will" rule 117
  who or Whom (when to use) 52–53

Run–on sentence 43

S

Sentences
  complex sentence 45–68
  compound sentence 37–44
  fragments 60
  simple sentence 5–36

Simple sentence 5–36
  diagramming simple sentences 6–36
  types of simple sentences 5
    declarative 5
    imperative 5
    interrogative 5
    exclamatory 5

Subject–Verb agreement 12–13

Subjective and objective complements 27–32

Subjective complement 27

    subjective complement types 29

        predicate adjective 29

        predicate nominative 30

    subjective complement identity test 28–29

V

Verbs 2, 99–123

    active and passive voice 108–110

        recognizing passive voice 109

    fast facts about verbs 23, 28

    forms and tenses 113–117

        irregular verbs 113–114

        regular verbs 113

        modes and Tenses (Guidelines) 120–123

        modes 118

            perfect and Progressive modes 120

            progressive modes of the verb "write" 119–120

        tenses 114–115

            conjugation of irregular verb "write" 119

    mood verbs 110–112

        imperative 110

        indicative 110

        subjunctive 110–111

            recognizing subjunctive mood 111–112

            understanding subjunctive mood 111

    number/Person verb agreement 106

        related to inverted sentences 107–108

rule: "Shall" or "will" 117

types of verbs:

    action verbs 100–101

        transitive verbs 100

        intransitive verbs 100

    helping (auxiliary) verbs 103–105

        modal verbs 105–106

    linking verbs 102–103

        "be" or "to be" verb 102

        sense perception verbs 102–103

Verbals 87–97

    gerund 87, 90–92

        diagramming gerunds and gerund phrases 91–92

    infinitive 87, 93–95

        infinitives functioning as nouns 93

        as adjectives and adverbs 93, 95

        diagramming infinitive phrases functioning as nouns 94

        as adjectives and adverbs 95

    participle 87–90

        present participle phrases 88

        past participle phrases 88

        diagramming participles and participle phrases 88–90

W

Who or whom? (understanding when to use) 83–84